Careers in Secret Operations

Foreign Intelligence Book Series

Thomas F. Troy, General Editor

Careers in Secret Operations
How to Be a Federal Intelligence Officer

David Atlee Phillips

A reliable guide for young men and women who contemplate an intelligence career and, for those who have made a decision, advice on how to find employment with the CIA, FBI, the Secret Service, the National Security Agency, and other government departments involved in secret operations.

University Publications of America, Inc.

University Publications of America, Inc.
44 North Market Street, Frederick, Maryland 21701

Copyright © 1984 by David Atlee Phillips

Library of Congress Cataloging in Publication Data

Phillips, David Atlee.
  Careers in secret operations.

  Bibliography: p. 89
    1. Intelligence officers—United States—Vocational
guidance.   2. Intelligence service—United States.
I. Title.
  UB251.U5P45   1984   327.1'2'02373   84-22009
  ISBN 0-89093-653-6

Printed in the United States of America

158195

Contents

Also by
David Atlee Phillips:

The Night Watch
The Carlos Contract
The Great Texas Murder Trials

Introduction

In the mid 1970s the U.S. intelligence community—the several agencies and departments that work with classified information and, in most cases, conduct secret operations—was subjected to a barrage of criticism, innuendo, and sensational media exposure. Intelligence officers found their previously romantic image tarnished. Central Intelligence Agency (CIA) and Federal Bureau of Investigation (FBI) agents were described by some and perceived by many as uncontrolled zealots, impervious to good judgment and engaged in every kind of trickery.

The new perception concerning those involved in espionage, counter-intelligence, and "dirty tricks" was understandable, perhaps inevitable in a post-Vietnam, post-Watergate America. It was healthy that questionable actions by an agency or its personnel that may have threatened the basic values of our country, especially the rights of American citizens, were the subject of intensive scrutiny by the Congress and the public. At times the heat of the investigations, however, was so searing that I feared the U.S. intelligence establishment, certainly already damaged, might have been crippled.

The debate over this country's clandestine operations reached its climax in 1975 in a high tide of confusion with the wreckage strewn over the Washington, D.C., landscape and on many foreign shores as well. Some criticisms of the seamy side of our intelligence agencies' behavior were deserved. Others were ill-founded but sincere. A small minority were the product of deliberate obfuscation, most often voiced by a clique of former intelligence officers who found the market for their knowledge of secret activities lucrative, especially if given a sensationalist tinge.

Any secret organization in a democratic society is a potential threat, but one, I am convinced, we must tolerate and control for the net gain. In May of 1975 I retired early from the CIA after twenty-five years as an intelligence officer, so I might be free to speak up for the "Silent Services" in the controversy over our nation's secret operations. One of my principal concerns was that young people contemplating a career in government might hesitate to be associated with the CIA, FBI, or the other intelligence services. I feared the effectiveness of the intelligence community would decline precipitously (and dangerously) without the infusion of new blood from young applicants fresh out of American colleges and universities. Replenishment of ideas and outlooks is vital to any organization, and especially so in the case of government bureaucracies. My fears, however, were ill-founded.

The development that precipitated the congressional investigations and the public brouhaha about the CIA was a front-page exposé by journalist Seymour Hersh in the *New York Times* of December 22, 1974. The accuracy of the Hersh story and his characterization of CIA involvement in domestic operations as "massive" was subsequently the subject of considerable, and sometimes acrimonious, debate. One thing was certain. The Hersh revelations produced massive cracks in what had been up to that time a fairly monolithic intelligence establishment. The question for the future was simple: Would qualified young people choose to become intelligence officers in the face of such a conglomeration of truths, half-truths, and plain untruths?

Immediately after the Hersh story was published the number of applications for CIA employment tripled.

Why? A tight job market, perhaps? A more plausible explanation, I decided, was to be derived from the refrain, "I don't care what you write about me as long as you spell my name correctly." Apparently, increasing numbers of young people sought an opportunity to work in the challenging business of intelligence simply because they had learned something about it for the first time; thus, today only those who survive intense competition obtain employment in government intelligence services.

Since retiring I have talked with hundreds of young people during college campus lectures or in connection with my work for the Association of Former Intelligence Officers, a national group of former intelligence men and women from all services. This volume answers the questions about intelligence asked of me in discussions with students or by young professionals considering switching from more mundane careers to intelligence work of one kind or another.

The intelligence trade is a demanding one, posing problems of morality and personal ethics for its practitioners. A heavy, green book published in Washington, D.C., in early 1976 and entitled *The Final Report of the Select Committee to Study Governmental Operations with Respect to Intelligence Activities* (better known as the Senate Church Committee Report) described it this way: "...in some respects, the intelligence profession resembles monastic life with some of the discipline and personal sacrifices reminiscent of medieval orders. Intelligence work is a life of service, but one in which the norms of American life are sometimes distressingly distorted."

Yet intelligence is reputed to be the second oldest profession. In the Bible we read that Moses sent his agents "to spy out the land of Canaan." Espionage techniques were refined by the Greeks and Romans and, of course, the Byzantines. The British intelligence service was created by Sir Francis Walsingham, Queen Elizabeth's secretary of state, and his fledgling spies proved their worth by penetrating the French and Spanish courts. One of his agents is said to have interrupted Sir Francis Drake's game of bowls in 1588 to give him the intelligence on the Spanish Armada approaching on the horizon. In France, Richelieu ran a proficient intelligence service. European bankers sponsored private espionage nets; the Rothschilds had one of the best. Every major European power conducted secret operations. Under Czar Nicholas I the Russians combined espionage with police repression, but Nicholas's service was puny in comparison with those that succeeded it. For example, the ubiquitous Soviet KGB, formally known as the Committee for State Security, employs more intelligence officers and spies today than all the other services of the world combined, and that is just one of the USSR's intelligence arms.

The 1771 edition of the *Encyclopedia Britannica* briefly depicted the secret agent as "SPY, a person hired to watch the actions, motions, etc. of another; particularly of what passes in a camp. When a spy is discovered he is hanged immediately." An early American agent, Nathan Hale, described intelligence as "a peculiar service." (Most definitions of *peculiar* in the dictionary mean funny, odd, strange. Hale was employing a British definition: "A particular parish or church exempted from the jurisdiction of the ordinary or bishop in whose diocese it lies and is governed by another.") Hale was a spy and was "hanged immediately" when his mission on Manhattan Island was uncovered in 1776.

Since Hale's days, young Americans have looked for a future of excitement and daring in intelligence careers. I give early warning: James Bond is fictional. Intelligence work often involves the accumulation and assembling of bits and pieces of information into a meaningful mosaic—a tedious business at times. One intelligence veteran once remarked that the truth would be better served if the cloak-and-dagger symbol for espionage were changed to that of a typewriter and some three-by-five cards.

But it is also true that on occasion American intelligence agents must act—and react—like James Bond at the barricades. Those who seek foreign adventure will want to work in the Directorate of Operations of the CIA, also known as the Clandestine Service. Or they can find action in one of the several military departments that engage in secret operations and undercover work; in the division of the FBI charged with monitoring and sometimes detaining foreign spies who operate in the United States; or, to a lesser degree, in special units of the Drug Enforcement Administration, U.S. Customs, and similar agencies. In any of these areas, intelligence officers and their agents must live double lives and face danger. It can be a tough way to make a living.

For the less adventuresome, satisfying careers await in the overt side of the intelligence profession. The majority of American intelligence officers and employees do not engage in covert or clandestine activities; they are scholars, analysts, administrators, investigators, communicators, and housekeeping personnel. Unlike their covert colleagues, they identify themselves to friends, neighbors, and credit unions as being associated with intelligence. They enjoy a more normal life-style which is not as demanding of spouses and children as that of the clandestine operative.

In whatever sphere, intelligence is a rewarding career for anyone dedicated to public service, and the personal satisfactions can be substantial. This book will attempt to answer the questions of those who contemplate an intelligence career and, for those who have decided to seek such an opportunity, to tell them how to go about entering the profession.

I
Questions and Answers
about Intelligence

I've been into drugs. Will I be hired?

It depends on the narcotic used, the frequency of use, and how recently you were into it. Experimental or on-and-off marijuana history will not faze interviewers. Depending on circumstances, hard drug habits long ago (such as during military service) may be overlooked. But prolonged use of any drug, including alcohol, will probably preclude employment. If you are hired by the CIA or the FBI, be ready to give up all narcotics.

Will I be asked embarrassing questions during a CIA lie detector test?

In a pre-employment examination, yes. And be prepared for periodic polygraph tests throughout your CIA career, but the questions become less personal.

What about fudging in the first examination? Can I beat the lie detector?

Probably not, unless you are a pathological liar. And that trait would be revealed during other tests you must undergo or during interviews with people who know you. The polygraph is only one facet of a security investigation.

If I flunk a security investigation, will I be told why?

Probably not.

I'm gay. Does it matter?

Yes. U.S. intelligence agencies and departments do not now hire known homosexuals. (However, see Chapter XII.)

I once had an experimental homosexual fling. Does that matter?

No.

1

How private is your private life?

Reasonably private. But if you begin hanging around with the Soviet embassy crowd, you will be investigated. Intelligence officers have private lives much like anyone else except for the demands of security. The FBI, while much more relaxed than in the past, does not tolerate two bureau employees living together who are not married.

If I work abroad under cover, can I ever become an ambassador?

Not unless you are on detached service from the CIA, with the rank of ambassador (as William Colby was during the Vietnam War), or unless you are appointed as an ambassador after you retire from the CIA (Richard Helms became the U.S. ambassador in Iran).

Does an American ambassador know the CIA people in the country?

Always, if they are Americans under official cover.

Can an ambassador prohibit a CIA station chief from sending an intelligence report to Washington?

No, but the ambassador must always be given the chance to comment on the message. Former CIA legislative counsel Walter L. Pforzheimer recalls a congressional investigation at which he was present in 1948. There had been a bloody uprising in Bogotá, Colombia, in which distinguished U.S. visitors were in jeopardy. The CIA knew in advance about the danger but was unable to warn Washington because the ambassador—at the insistence of a Department of State advance man—refused to send the message. Since then, CIA stations can insist an intelligence report be forwarded despite an ambassador's objection.

Must American deep-cover agents abroad pay U.S. income tax? If so, how do they do it without blowing their cover?

All Americans working for U.S. intelligence, wherever they are, must pay income tax. This sometimes requires the preparation of a special return that goes to a cleared unit of the Internal Revenue Service.

Can I write for publication?

You will be encouraged to write for publication in your field of expertise if you are an overt employee of a U.S. intelligence organization. Your employer will want to review the material for security reasons. Special rules apply if you are under cover. E. Howard Hunt published several dozen spy novels under various pseudonyms during his CIA career.

Isn't signing a secrecy oath—promising to submit everything I write even after I retire—prior restraint and thus unconstitutional?

The Supreme Court has ruled that secrecy oaths signed by government employees are valid civil contracts. If you work in a General Electric research laboratory, you will be required to sign a similar agreement promising not to reveal trade secrets when you retire or go to work for another company. A secrecy oath cannot be used to stifle criticism or opinion. It can be invoked only if real secrets are involved, especially the revelation of sources and methods (who or what provides information, and how).

What about moonlighting?

A second or part-time occupation is discouraged in the intelligence community at home, and is not tolerated abroad. In Washington, D.C., your career will suffer if your duty officer cannot find you because, as a weekend realtor, you are out selling a house. If the work spills over into office hours, you will be chastised.

I understand there are CIA offices in most major American cities. How do I locate them?

You can find domestic CIA offices in the phone book.

As a woman, will I be asked to use sex in intelligence work?

No. When cultivating a prospective agent, you will use a reasonable amount of charm in the process as a man will. But I know of no case where an American woman intelligence officer was asked to sleep with a potential agent, or where a female officer allowed herself to lose the authority and control essential to managing an agent by sharing his bed.

How dangerous is intelligence work?

Spies—foreigners in the employ of U.S. intelligence—lead a dangerous life. They are often arrested and imprisoned, and sometimes executed. American intelligence officers in deep-cover assignments in some countries face risks. Those in official cover in a U.S. overseas installation once lived reasonably safe lives, but peril has escalated in recent years due to terrorist bombings and kidnapings of U.S. military and diplomatic personnel.

In the United States the work of FBI agents, especially apprehending criminals, can be dangerous. Secret Service agents guarding a president never know when they will have to stand between him and an assassin's bullet. The most dangerous of all intelligence/investigative work is in the Drug Enforcement Administration (DEA), particularly when DEA agents are sent on foreign assignments.

Will I use and carry a gun?

FBI, DEA, and Secret Service agents carry guns and sometimes use them. CIA agents seldom carry weapons and rarely use them. With the exception of the employees of the Department of State's Bureau of Analysis and Research and the National Security Agency, all U.S. intelligence officers are trained in the use of weapons.

Is it true that undercover agents and their families must lead double lives?

It goes with the territory. Concealing the truth is a necessary part of getting the job done overseas. And, to sustain cover, a life of duplicity must continue during tours in U.S. headquarters. An undercover agent must lie to his neighbors, his banker, and to most relatives. It's not pleasant, but it is essential.

How much do intelligence officers tell their spouses?

They keep their spouses briefed on what they are doing without going into detail. Even teen-age children, depending on circumstances and the maturity of the child, are told that their father or mother is an intelligence officer.

Why are intelligence people called "spooks"?

Spook is the term often used by foreign service officers when referring to CIA colleagues. Sometimes the term is used pejoratively and sometimes affectionately. CIA officers have learned to live with the name and occasionally refer to themselves as spooks.

Is a college degree essential for intelligence work?

The FBI, CIA, and National Security Agency insist on a degree for entry level employees who will be officers. Some agencies, such as the Secret Service, recognize work experience equivalents in lieu of a degree. Degrees are not required for military officers or for agents of the Drug Enforcement Administration. (Many employees of all agencies become officers after working in low-level positions until they can obtain night school degrees.)

How many "moles" are there in the CIA?

We would not know, of course, of a truly successful mole. But despite much speculation—some sensational in nature—there is no evidence that a mole has ever burrowed into the CIA at the staff level. (William Kampiles and David Barnett approached the Soviets to sell information and service after they left the CIA. Philip Agee is another former CIA employee who began his mischief after resigning. In the press, he has identified hundreds of intelligence officers. His book, *Inside the Company: A CIA Diary*, was written with the assistance of the Cuban Communist party.)

Why hasn't the CIA assassinated Philip Agee?

Two past CIA plots to kill men other than Agee misfired, so the agency seems to be clumsy when trying to assassinate. It is doubtful the CIA would attempt such action after the headlines that erupted during the Church Committee investigations. Certainly Agee would not be a target. Should a truck run over him tomorrow, the CIA will undoubtedly be blamed for the accident.

If I work for the CIA, will I ever be asked to kill anyone?

An executive order now prohibits assassination. However, things might be different in wartime.

Are James Bond adventure books accurate?

No.

Do undercover families have higher divorce, alcoholism, and suicide rates?

Divorce and alcoholism statistics are slightly higher than the national average. Suicides are less than the normal figure.

Can I refuse an intelligence assignment I don't like?

You can always get out of an overseas assignment with a valid reason, such as needing special medical attention for a family member. Otherwise, the FBI, the Secret Service, and all the military services will expect you to move when asked. In the CIA you can probably manage to turn down an undesirable assignment once. Challenging the wisdom of the hierarchy a second time without valid medical or family reasons tends to "stifle upward career mobility."

What if I decide, after trying it, that I want to quit?

It is not easy to quit the military until your period of enlistment is completed. Other government agencies and departments require only two weeks' notice. (If you quit during the first year of an overseas assignment, you must reimburse the government for all travel and transport to and from that area.)

What if I want time to think things over?

In most government agencies, you can usually get a year away from the job without pay.

Do intelligence officers receive overtime pay?

It depends on the agency. All of them pay overtime to lower-level employees. Special agents in the FBI are paid overtime, but most other agencies do not pay middle- and senior-grade personnel for extra work.

Hazardous duty or hardship allowances are paid to U.S. personnel overseas, especially during periods of prolonged civil strife.

Do intelligence officers receive special retirement benefits?

Department of State officers, FBI special agents, and CIA people who have spent at least five years abroad receive retirement benefits that are slightly better than the Civil Service retirement circumstances of other government workers. (You should know the details of a retirement system before your money goes into it. But when discussing employment with an intelligence organization, keep queries about retirement in low key. Otherwise, veterans considering your employment will mutter about motivation.)

My future wife wants a career of her own and has told me she will not accompany me overseas. What about her?

The problem has become a serious one in recent years. In most countries, wives cannot obtain working permits. The only satisfactory solution so far is when the Department of State and the CIA send husband-wife teams overseas, which they do more frequently these days.

Does specializing in intelligence in the military hurt promotion chances?

Yes. Most military intelligence officers realize they will not become generals or admirals if they remain in intelligence throughout a career.

Who watches the CIA?

Until recently, eight committees in Congress handled the job. That didn't work because you can't conduct secret operations in Bloomingdale's window. Now the CIA reports to one committee in the Senate and a second one in the House of Representatives. This is more reasonable, but still not ideal, considering the continued leakage from the committees as well as the administration.

Do CIA officers receive medals or decorations?

Yes. The highest tribute is the Distinguished Intelligence Cross awarded for valor. The Distinguished Intelligence Medal is the best awarded for performance. CIA medals are kept in a safe at Langley, Virginia, until the officer honored retires or resigns. In some cases, to protect a cover mechanism, the decoration is never turned over to the officer.

Do CIA people really call the agency "the Company"?

Yes. And some call it "the Pickle Factory."

I've seen ads in the New York Times *asking people to apply to the CIA. Do intelligence agencies in other countries use want ads to seek recruits?*

It could only happen in America. The CIA is not the only intelligence agency that advertises for employees. The Defense Intelligence Agency recently did so, and even the supersecret National Security Agency (NSA) has used newspaper recruitment. Recently the NSA conducted a Jobs Fair to which it invited those people interested in becoming codebreakers. But foreign intelligence organizations don't advertise. A visiting British intelligence man, seeing the ads in the *Washington Post*, commented, "I am totally astonished."

II
Applying for the Job—
How, Where, and When

First, you must obtain and complete an application form. A *formidable* form! Formidable is an adjective from the Latin, and its definitions include "Causing fear, dread, or apprehension...having qualities that discourage approach...tending to inspire awe or wonder." That's a precise description of the forms required by intelligence agencies from prospective employees.

The CIA has traditionally insisted that candidates complete a Personal History Statement (PHS), Parts One and Two. Very recently the questionnaire has been somewhat simplified and reduced to a single PHS. It remains, however, a compendium of answers about your life, your places of residence, employment, education, associates, personal habits, health, and so on.

Several U.S. intelligence organizations require completion of a U.S. Government Standard Form 171 which, while not as formidable as the CIA PHS, is still a grueling chore to finish. The U.S. Treasury has its own application called the Treasury Enforcement Agency Examination. Whatever the agency or department, the form is an arduous one. If it is any consolation, filling out the form will pay off in the long run; it forces you to gather together all the personal information about yourself (e.g., where you have lived, what elementary school you attended, where your father was born) that you will likely need at some future time to satisfy some other prospective employer.

Applications for employment and literature about job opportunities and entry requirements may be obtained by writing to the national headquarters of the agency involved. For example:

Director of Personnel
Central Intelligence Agency
Washington, D.C. 20505

9

Director
Federal Bureau of Investigation
Washington, D.C. 20535

United States Secret Service
Personnel Division
1800 G Street, NW
Washington, D.C. 20223

If you have a particular area of interest, however, it is best to contact specific offices. As you will shortly read, the chapters in this book about CIA employment provide several different mailing addresses for those with specialized backgrounds.

Application forms may also be obtained throughout the United States in regional and local offices of the various services. A personal visit to pick up the forms sometimes establishes a relationship that will be useful in treading through the bureaucratic maze. These local addresses are also listed in the appropriate chapters of this volume.

College and university students may obtain application forms and detailed descriptions of job openings from campus recruiters. CIA recruiters, who retreated from on-campus recruiting during the years of fervid controversy about secret operations, have reappeared at most schools to seek employees. Even the National Security Agency—the U.S. codebreaking establishment— now recruits new talent from college campuses.

Young people who contemplate careers in intelligence should apply in the final year of college or immediately after graduation. Generalists in security agencies—such as CIA case officers and FBI special agents—are recruited among youthful prospects, and the competition is tight and the time required for security clearances is lengthy. Therefore, applications should be submitted as early as possible.

Specialists with skills in science and technology are sought by intelligence organizations regardless of age; therefore, more mature applicants considering career changes are encouraged to apply.

GOVERNMENT EMPLOYMENT BENEFITS AND PAY

The benefits for federal employees are an important consideration for those who weigh the difference between careers in the private sector and the government. As a rule, government treats its people well.

Most U.S. government workers are members of the Civil Service Retirement System. Those with at least five years of federal civilian service who become disabled through job-related disease or injury may apply for early disability retirement. Also, if an employee dies before becoming eligible for retirement but after eighteen months' civilian service, the surviving spouse (if married to the employee at least one year or if the parent of a child of the marriage) and eligible children under eighteen years of age (or twenty-two if attending school) become entitled to certain benefits which begin immediately on the death of the employee.

Federal employees receive thirteen working days' annual paid vacation during the first three years on the job, and twenty working days annually thereafter until they have served the government for fifteen years (including military service) after which time they receive twenty-six days of paid vacation. Unused annual leave can be accumulated up to a maximum of thirty working days. There are also sick leave benefits enabling an employee to be absent from duty because of illness without loss of pay or vacation time.

Health and life insurance policies for all U.S. government employees are relatively inexpensive, and the coverage is good. All government agencies have credit unions for their people, and membership in them may be continued after retirement.

Those employees involved in certain fields of intelligence work, criminal investigation, or foreign service are covered by retirement benefits that allow early retirement. Special agents in the FBI, for instance, may retire at age fifty with a minimum of twenty years' service. CIA officers who serve at least five years overseas have the same early retirement option.

Most federal employees are paid under what is known as the Government Service Pay Scale (the GS). The lowest current annual salary in this system is for GS-01 employees, whose jobs are those of an undemanding nature. The highest salary is for GS-18 officers, who have reached the highest position possible except for presidential appointees.

Uniformed members of the military intelligence services are paid, of course, according to their rank, from private to general.

A comparison with military wages is perhaps the easiest way to understand the complicated GS pay schedule which is used by most (but not all) of the civilian agencies and departments. Workers in the GS-01 through GS-08 rank can be compared with enlisted military personnel, private through top sergeant. The officer ranks in the GS schedule begin at GS-09 (lieutenant) to GS-15 (lieutenant colonel) in the junior- and middle-grade levels. Once a civilian becomes a supergrader (GS-16 through GS-18), he or she is the equivalent of a military full colonel or general.

In short, the civilian government employee strives to obtain the highest number possible. An exception is the seniority rating of Department of State foreign service officers, who work to achieve the lowest number they can, FSO-1.

Currently, ninety-nine out of every one hundred white-collar federal workers get a within-grade pay raise each time they become eligible through a specified length of service. Depending on their time in a particular grade, workers come due for a step increase every one, two, or three years. The raises are worth about 3 percent of one's salary.

Pay scales for government employees, civilian and military, increase periodically with across-the-board raises in accordance with raises in the official cost-of-living index.

The chart below (valid at the time of writing) can be used to identify the actual sum you will be paid once employed. If you are advised that you will begin duty as a GS-07, for example, see Longevity Step 1 for the annual salary for a GS-07 just aboard.

A word of warning for your future, senior years of service. Salaries are "frozen" at a certain level, tied to the wages members of Congress vote for themselves. Therefore, a GS-16 officer may receive the same salary as his GS-17 and GS-18 supervisors.

1984 Pay Schedule for Federal White-collar Workers

Step	1	2	3	4	5	6	7	8	9	10
GS										
1	$ 9,023	$ 9,324	$ 9,624	$ 9,924	$10,224	$10,400	$10,697	$10,995	$11,008	$11,283
2	10,146	10,386	10,722	11,008	11,129	11,456	11,783	12,110	12,437	12,764
3	11,070	11,439	11,808	12,177	12,546	12,915	13,284	13,653	14,022	14,391
4	12,427	12,841	13,255	13,669	14,083	14,497	14,911	15,325	15,739	16,153
5	13,903	14,366	14,829	15,292	15,755	16,218	16,681	17,144	17,607	18,070
6	15,497	16,014	16,531	17,048	17,565	18,082	18,599	19,116	19,633	20,150
7	17,221	17,795	18,369	18,943	19,517	20,091	20,665	21,239	21,813	22,387
8	19,073	19,709	20,345	20,981	21,617	22,253	22,889	23,525	24,161	24,797
9	21,066	21,768	22,470	23,172	23,874	24,576	25,278	25,980	26,682	27,384
10	23,199	23,972	24,745	25,518	26,291	27,064	27,837	28,610	29,383	30,156
11	25,489	26,339	27,189	28,039	28,889	29,739	30,589	31,439	32,289	33,139
12	30,549	31,567	32,585	33,603	34,621	35,639	36,657	37,675	38,693	39,711
13	36,327	37,538	38,749	39,960	41,171	42,382	43,593	44,804	46,015	47,226
14	42,928	44,359	45,790	47,221	48,652	50,083	51,514	52,945	54,376	55,807
15	50,495	52,178	53,861	55,544	57,227	58,910	60,593	62,276	63,959	65,642
16	59,223	61,197	63,171	65,145	67,119*	69,093*	71,067*	73,041*	75,015*	
17	69,376*	71,689*	74,002*	76,315*	78,628*					
18	81,311*									

*The rate of basic pay payable to employes at these rates is limited to the rate payable for level V of the Executive Schedule, $66,400.

Source: Office of Personnel Management

WHERE THE JOBS ARE

The CIA has received so much publicity that it is often mistakenly presumed to be the only organization in which a career in intelligence can be pursued. Not so. The United States has what is called "the intelligence community," a loose grouping of a number of federal agencies, each of which has a part to play in intelligence. These agencies include the FBI; the NSA; the Defense Intelligence Agency (DIA); army, navy, air force, and marine intelligence; the Treasury Department; the Secret Service; the U.S. Customs Service; the DEA; and the Bureau of Alcohol, Tobacco, and Firearms.

The chapters that follow discuss each of these agencies. Read them with an open mind; that is, do not decide beforehand that one agency is more interesting or less interesting than another. The best course of action would be to find out what kinds of people are being sought by what agencies (in general, they are all looking for administrators, analysts, operators, secretaries, and so on), and then focus your attention on the organizations that would be most interested in someone of your particular interests, goals, and qualifications.

III
The Central Intelligence Agency

In 1950 in Santiago, Chile, a man I had previously known only as a diplomat in the American embassy asked me if I would "help out Uncle Sam" as a part-time agent of the CIA.

"The CIA?" I asked. "What's that?"

At one time the CIA was the *least* known of U.S. government agencies. In recent years CIA has become a household acronym.

The genesis of public support for the CIA was in the Japanese attack on Honolulu in 1941. The surprise at Pearl Harbor should not have been a surprise at all. It was a classic example of what happens when there is no *central* intelligence mechanism. Pearl Harbor was an inevitable intelligence failure because of a disparate intelligence community.

American cryptologists had broken "Purple" (the Japanese diplomatic code) and were deciphering coded messages months before the attack on Hawaii. Pres. Franklin Roosevelt and his advisors had studied more than two hundred Japanese cables and dispatches. The FBI eavesdropped on telephone conversations between Japanese diplomats in Washington and Japan and, on December 6, 1941, on the conversation of a spy in Honolulu reporting on shipping during a call to Tokyo. Japanese military leaders made bellicose speeches laced with threats and, on one occasion, predicted war with America. One speech was so inflammatory that Secretary of State Cordell Hull called President Roosevelt back to Washington from a Warm Springs, Georgia, vacation. A Yugoslavian playboy (and British-sponsored double agent), Dusko Popov, arrived in New York four months before Pearl Harbor. He was a colorful spy, said to have been the model for the fictional Agent 007, James Bond. His lifestyle was so flamboyant that a myth was perpetuated that the autocratic and strait-laced director of the FBI, J. Edgar Hoover, rebuffed him as irresponsible and dismissed his information about Japanese plans to attack Pearl Harbor. In fact, the FBI did obtain his story.

15

Not one of these indicators—or several others—alone provided hard intelligence of when and where the Japanese would attack, but had all the reports been evaluated and collated collectively, a clear warning would have emerged from the analysis.

When the United States entered the war after Pearl Harbor, its intelligence capabilities were in pitiful disarray. So little was known about our enemies that Americans who had been tourists overseas before the war were asked to send in the snapshots they had taken of European and Far Eastern cities, beaches, ports, highways, and canals. In July 1941, President Roosevelt asked New York lawyer William J. Donovan to form the Office of Strategic Services (OSS). The OSS became an efficient wartime intelligence group. It supplied policymakers with essential facts and estimates and often played a vital role in directly supporting military campaigns. But the OSS did not have jurisdiction over all foreign intelligence activities. The FBI conducted espionage tasks in Latin America, and the military services protected their own areas of responsibility.

After World War II, Pres. Harry Truman recognized the need for a central intelligence organization. And in 1947, after a few predecessor agencies functioned briefly, Truman and Congress created the CIA. Many of the original CIA officers had learned about clandestine operations during OSS service. The 1947 National Security Act authorized these men and women to engage in "services of common concern"—to conduct espionage— and to evaluate and disseminate the information they gathered from secret sources. They were to work with other intelligence agencies, domestic and foreign. The act also instructed them "to perform such other functions and duties" as might be required "from time to time." That vague phrase I call the Great Big Banana Peel. It was perceived by some as a charter for the CIA to conduct covert action: secret operations abroad, usually political in nature, designed to influence events and provide U.S. presidents with an option between an ineffective diplomatic protest and sending in the marines. During twenty years of cold war with the Soviet Union, some CIA covert actions were immensely successful; others were highly publicized failures. There will always be controversy about whether the CIA should engage in covert action. But, despite the questions of morality involved, it is highly unlikely that U.S. presidents and secretaries of state will abandon it entirely as a political option.

Because of its unique responsibilities and demanding assignments, the CIA attempts to recruit personnel of the highest quality. The vast majority of those who are employed in three of the agency's four directorates will serve out their careers in the CIA's Langley, Virginia, headquarters as analysts, scientists, or administrators. Those applicants who enter the CIA's Directorate of Operations as case officers—managers of spies—must be prepared to further their education at the CIA's school, known as "the Farm." It is specialized postgraduate study with an arcane curriculum. They must further be prepared to spend most of their careers in challenging overseas assignments. In the foreign service, *challenging* can mean anything from an exciting tour in an international hot spot to enduring bad plumbing and insect swarms in a remote outpost.

HOW APPLICANTS ARE INVESTIGATED BY THE CIA

A lie detector test will be administered for those seeking employment with the CIA, and some of the questions will be disturbing. The polygraph examination is only one of a number of probes into your psyche and private life. These invasions of your privacy can be disconcerting; but you are not, after all, joining the Boy Scouts.

Some intelligence services do not require such thorough scrutiny of prospective employees. The British services, according to newspaper reports in England, shun the polygraph—which may explain why there have been a first, second, third, fourth and, perhaps, a fifth man uncovered in Her Majesty's Secret Intelligence Service as Soviet moles. Despite speculation to the contrary, there has never been a proven case of a mole burrowed in the CIA, probably due to the in-depth investigation of CIA applicants.

CIA background investigations are brief only when the applicant has already been partially cleared because of a family connection or service with another agency or department of the U.S. government. Normally, CIA background checks take several months.

First, there is a full field investigation. FBI checks are conducted on the applicant and his or her spouse, as well as the parents if the applicant is under twenty-one years of age. Office of Personnel Management (formerly the Civil Service Commission) records are reviewed along with those of other agencies, such as the Department of Defense Central Index of Investigations and the Immigration and Naturalization Service. The field investigation covers the most recent fifteen years of the applicant's life or from age seventeen, whichever is briefer. Birth is verified in order to establish identity, parentage, and citizenship. An applicant must have been a U.S. citizen for at least five years, and his or her spouse must be a citizen. And, CIA hopefuls should have no relative or person to whom they are bound by close ties of affection or obligation subject to a foreign power.

Your education, work history, and places of residence are checked; neighbors are interviewed in most cases. Police records are reviewed at places where you have lived, worked, or attended school. Credit reputation is established through credit checks and reporting agencies. A minimum of five character references, including peers, are interviewed. A mass of personal data is explored—information previously supplied on the employment application form.

When all the investigative studies are completed the applicant is scheduled for a polygraph examination. While not infallible, the lie detector test in the hands of expert CIA examiners is invaluable in validating investigative information and exploring issues of security relevance with the applicant. Polygraph questions are reviewed prior to the actual examination. (And the polygraph operator will assure you, probably accurately, that you cannot tell him anything he has not heard before.)

In analyzing everything they learn about an applicant, the CIA pays special attention to potential vulnerability to exploitation by hostile intelligence services (i.e., being susceptible to blackmail). Sexual perversion, dishonesty, immoral or notoriously disgraceful conduct, and conviction of felonious or serious misdemeanor criminal acts are considered highly significant. Use or abuse of drugs, including marijuana, will be examined. Depending on circumstances, past use of drugs does not preclude CIA employment.

A decision to grant or deny a CIA security clearance is made only after a full review of all pertinent information developed in the security processing. Any disapproval recommendation must pass several levels of review before the matter is presented to the CIA's director of security for a final decision.

THE FOUR CIA DIRECTORATES

The director of Central Intelligence (DCI) is the senior U.S. intelligence officer holding cabinet rank. The chiefs of all other services report through him to the White House and the National Security Council. The DCI also acts as head of the CIA, which consists of four departments known as directorates: the Directorate of Intelligence, known as the Deputy Director, Intelligence (DDI); the Directorate of Administration, known as the Deputy Director, Administration (DDA); the Directorate of Science and Technology, known as the Deputy Director, Science and Technology (DDS&T); and the Directorate of Operations, known as the Deputy Director, Operations (DDO), and which is also known as the Clandestine Service (CS) (until 1973, the DDO was called the Deputy Director, Plans, or DDP).

Each directorate is composed of branches, offices, units, or groups, and they are described in the following pages. The names of these offices occasionally change during internal reorganizations; functions, however, remain the same in the renamed office, unless they are transferred to another.

THE DIRECTORATE OF INTELLIGENCE—DDI

In 1965 Pres. Lyndon Johnson startled Washington, including those of us at the CIA, by sending 22,000 American troops into the Dominican Republic. Johnson wanted to know what was going on in Santo Domingo, now! We started putting out situation reports every hour, twenty-four hours a day. At Langley, DDI officers worked directly with officers of the clandestine DDO. I was at a desk with a DDI officer across from me and together we prepared the hourly situation reports that were flashed to the White House, State, Defense, USIA, and half a dozen other agencies.

The Office of Economic Research (OER) is a major component of the Directorate of Intelligence. Its principal task is to conduct research, analyze, and write reports on significant economic activities of foreign countries and regional groups in support of the formulation and execution of United States policy. The CIA analyst working in the OER studies those current and potential foreign economic developments that can affect the vital interests of the United States—economic, security, and other. Assignments are varied and demanding. Responsibility comes early to the analyst who demonstrates the capability to handle it.

OER's most important customers are the president and policy-level officials in the executive staffs (National Security Council, Office of Management and Budget, Council of Economic Advisors) and the Departments of State, Treasury, Defense, Commerce, Agriculture, and Energy. Research support for these officials is designed to provide timely, thorough, and objective appraisals of foreign economic developments. Many reports are produced to fulfill a developing policy need. Papers vary in scope, from interpretive reporting on current events to comprehensive studies, such as the long-term impact on developed countries of high oil prices.

New OER analysts work with professional economists in representing practically all the major specialties within the field of economics. The keynote of personal relations between junior and veteran researchers is mutual interest and assistance. There is a spirit of competition among researchers in the best traditions of academic excellence. In most cases, the senior members of OER have had experience in a wide variety of geographical and functional areas of research. Supervisors are selected competitively. A person who lacks the skill or inclination for management has the opportunity to rise to a high-paying position on the basis of superior individual research.

The first assignment for a new OER analyst is usually to research one of many geographical or functional areas, and independent responsibility for a particular country or activity is given as soon as he or she demonstrates the ability to handle the subject. Essentially, the economic research analyst in the CIA uses the same skills as those employed in writing a graduate-level term paper or a journal article. Compared with the academic researchers, however, he or she is faced with stricter deadlines, a hierarchical system of review, and the necessity to preserve secrecy.

The OER is steadily moving into new analytical techniques, and offers opportunities for training in econometrics and computer applications. The CIA has one of the best scientific computer centers in the world, as well as programmers to assist analysts in drawing on extensive sets of programs and data bases for constructing and running econometric models.

While OER employees must maintain secrecy with regard to their sources of information, they are not covert CIA agents. They identify themselves to friends and neighbors as CIA employees. The CIA encourages OER people to maintain and broaden their professional ties through study, contacts with other persons and organizations engaged in economic research of mutual interests, attendance at professional meetings, teaching and lecturing in their field of expertise, and writing for publication in professional journals. Local universities offer a variety of graduate courses in economics, and analysts are encouraged to pursue additional study; moreover, the CIA usually pays the cost of after-hours economics courses. Also of importance to professional development is the emphasis placed on visits to industrial plants and agricultural stations and, where possible, to the foreign country on which the analyst is working.

The OER primarily seeks economist candidates with M.A. or Ph.D. degrees but will consider applicants with B.A. degrees if they possess exceptionally strong academic credentials. Salaries range from GS-07 through GS-14 depending on qualifications. Specialties usually required include industrial economics, agricultural economics, econometrics, petroleum economics, transportation economics, international trade and monetary developments, and economics of foreign countries.

The Office of Political Analysis (OPA) produces both quick-response and long-term, in-depth analyses of present and emerging foreign affairs problems of importance to United States policymakers and the intelligence community. New analysts assigned to OPA will be expected to enhance their knowledge of a country, region, or global issue; to conduct research— often multidisciplinary in nature—on important foreign intelligence problems; and to develop current intelligence assessments and briefings on fast-breaking international situations of vital interest to the national security of the United States.

OPA prefers individuals with M.A. or Ph.D. degrees in foreign history, political science, or international relations. An excellent academic record and a demonstrated interest in foreign affairs are prerequisites. Skill in written and oral presentation is a necessity. A willingness to work long hours during crisis periods is also expected. The beginning salary range is from GS-09 through GS-12.

The OPA is able to provide considerable support to analysts in the form of research assistants, bibliographic searches, access to the holdings of the Library of Congress, and the benefit of overseas reporting (including information from spies) as well as information from other, more esoteric (highly classified) sources. Continued contact with the academic community is encouraged. OPA analysts frequently present papers at academic conferences and publish unclassified research. Rotational assignments to other components of the CIA or government agencies are often approved. Such assignments are viewed as an important means of broadening an individual's analytical horizons and enhancing career development. There are also occasional opportunities for travel and overseas assignments.

The Office of Strategic Research (OSR) supports national policymakers by preparing studies on foreign military programs and activities. Analysts draw on comprehensive and often unique sources to conduct in-depth research on the military philosophy and strength of selected countries, the relationship between economic resources and military programs, the effectiveness of military forces, and comparisons of military power.

The OSR is interested in applicants who have graduate or undergraduate degrees and who have demonstrated the ability to do in-depth research in one of the following disciplines: foreign area studies, political science, history, international relations, international business, economics or econometrics, or operations research.

Essential requirements for employment in the OSR are intellectual curiosity, analytical skill, and ability to write clearly and concisely on complex subjects. Certain positions require a strong statistical or data processing background. A knowledge of military weapons and operations is desirable. New analysts will acquire specific expertise through training courses and by working with experienced analysts. Starting salaries range from GS-07 through GS-13.

The Office of Central Reference (OCR) supports the Directorate of Intelligence analysts who produce intelligence for policymakers. It designs, develops, and operates reference facilities; receives and disseminates incoming intelligence reports and publications; provides remote terminal access to classified and unclassified information systems within the intelligence community, other government offices, and private industry; operates special libraries; coordinates procurement of publications; and produces biographic studies and files on foreign leaders and organizations.

Librarians hired by the OCR have entry salaries from GS-08 to GS-09. An offer of GS-10 or GS-11 will occasionally be made to someone with unusual credentials in the library field. An M.L.S. degree is required. Some reading proficiency in one or more foreign languages and some information science training or experience are desirable.

Area specialists' duties include writing reports on foreign leaders and providing answers to a wide variety of questions by doing research in manual and computer-based files. The resources available are vast, work is heavily influenced by world events, and the pressure of deadlines is constant. The starting salary for someone with a master's degree is GS-08. A master's degree with emphasis on area study is desired, but a bachelor's degree (e.g., political science) with a focal area plus relevant experience (overseas residence, military intelligence work, etc.) will be considered. In addition, Ph.D. graduates or candidates with a strong focus in biographic research or reference work may also be considered. Ability to write clearly and rapidly is essential; applicants will be asked to prepare a written sample during an initial interview. Interest in information storage and retrieval and an ability to read one or more foreign languages are highly desirable.

General liberal arts majors are employed by the OCR to serve as document analysts. Their duties include scanning a high volume of information reports, identifying key topics and concepts contained in them, and storing the marked data in a machine-retrievable data base. They also work as junior librarians engaged in the worldwide procurement of books, newspapers, and magazines. A keen ability to comprehend what they read, excellent vocabulary, and a good knowledge of current events are essential. A bachelor's degree in one of the liberal arts, particularly with concentration in foreign area study, political science, history, or a foreign language, is preferred; library science and information science graduates are also considered.

Computer scientists are employed by the OCR for unique information-handling and text-processing applications. Hardware used includes both large-scale CPUs and special-function minicomputer systems. A background in computer operation, data entry, and production control is useful, but hands-on programming experience is particularly valuable. Programmer applicants must pass the Brandon-Wolfe Programming Aptitude Test (OCR schedules this test for the initial interview). Starting salary is GS-07 for a person without experience but with proven programming ability or aptitude; relevant experience could qualify for a beginning GS-08 salary or higher. A bachelor's degree in data processing or a related field is highly desirable. At least the applicant should have relevant courses in the computer science/data processing field, such as system architecture, COBOL, FORTRAN, assembler language, or operating systems.

The Office of Geographic and Cartographic Research (OGCR) produces geographic intelligence and is composed of four major components.

The Environment and Resource Analysis Center performs interdisciplinary analyses in the fields of agriculture, food, population, water, energy, and minerals. The center produces reports incorporating the political, economic, and social implications of foreign resource and environmental issues. Jobs available include agro-economists, rice agronomists, demographers, ocean resource specialists, nonfuel minerals specialists, and operational research personnel.

The Geography Division produces regionally oriented geographic intelligence on issues of priority policy and strategic significance, including analysis of ethnic conflicts, territorial disputes and boundary problems, military geography, and the resource base. Job openings here are for geographers with foreign area expertise; candidates with foreign language capabilities are particularly employable.

The Cartographic Division provides cartographic and graphic services to the CIA and the Department of State. Jobs are open for cartographers, research geographers, graphics designers, and visual information specialists. Of particular interest are those candidates with strong academic backgrounds and/or portfolios that relate to computerized cartomation or graphics systems.

The Map Library Division collects and distributes maps to the CIA and other members of the intelligence community. Geographers and cartographers are hired, as well as librarians with strong foreign area interests.

The OGCR also has some positions for social demographers, cultural anthropologists, and other social scientists with foreign area expertise; foreign language capability is a plus.

Starting salaries in OGCR range from GS-07 to GS-12 depending on academic background and experience. Most professionals hired have a master's degree, but a few have a bachelor's degree or a Ph.D. Broad work experience, teaching experience, and foreign travel are also important considerations.

The Office of Imagery Analysis (OIA) offers employment to people who produce intelligence from the analysis of imagery (i.e., experts in aerial photography). Such intelligence is often vital for U.S. policymakers and military leaders (as it was to Pres. John F. Kennedy during the Cuban Missile Crisis of 1962). The work involves the surveillance of the organization and deployment of military forces; industrial production capacities and technology; and the development, testing, and production of new weapons systems. Most of the work requires in-depth, detailed analysis of subjects related to long-term key intelligence issues. But imagery analysts are also expected to react quickly to crises arising from the world's rapidly changing political climate. Imagery experts extract facts from photographs and correlate them with data from other sources. Conclusions reached and intelligence judgments made are either published in reports or presented at briefings. Analysts often serve as members of the CIA and intelligence community working groups.

The OIA neophytes are not expected to have extensive experience in intelligence applications of imagery. Their academic backgrounds cover as wide a spectrum as do the topics on which they work. Usually they are qualified people with bachelor's and master's degrees in geology, geography, civil engineering, and the physical and biological sciences. New analysts receive on-the-job training and some formal schooling, including a fifteen-week familiarization course. Starting salaries are GS-07 through GS-09.

The Office of Scientific and Weapons Research (OSWR) is responsible for determining the nature and scope of foreign scientific and technical activities and programs, and the performance capabilities of foreign weapons and space systems.

OSWR's analysts perform in-depth research and prepare reports for policymakers. Specific areas of research and analysis include science policy, the physical and life sciences, civil and military technology, nuclear energy and weapons, nuclear proliferation, offensive and defensive weapons systems, general purpose weapons, antisubmarine warfare, and space systems.

OSWR seeks persons with B.S. and M.S. degrees in material sciences, metallurgy, physics, chemistry, life sciences, physiology, mathematics, and aerospace, civil, chemical, electrical, and nuclear engineering. OSWR is also interested in those with Ph.D. degrees in nuclear engineering, electrical engineering, and physics, as well as in biophysics, biochemistry, and psychology.

Starting salaries at the OSWR range from GS-07 through GS-14 depending on qualifications and experience.

The Foreign Broadcast Information Service (FBIS) offers career opportunities for persons interested in foreign affairs who want to live and work abroad in positions that require timely reporting. FBIS monitors foreign public media (radio, television, newspapers, and journals) at a number of overseas field bureaus. Information of interest to policymakers is selected, translated, and transmitted by teletype. In Washington, D.C., the most urgent information is flashed to key officials on the FBIS wire service. The bulk of the product, however, is published in the FBIS *Daily Report* which is distributed to a variety of public officials and is sold to the public through the Department of Commerce.

FBIS information officers begin their careers in Washington as apprentice editors of the *Daily Report*. They undergo a training program lasting up to eighteen months, which combines formal instruction and on-the-job training, climaxed by a twelve-week assignment to an overseas field bureau. FBIS officers learn copyediting, style and format, selection that is responsive to consumer requirement, organization and presentation and, finally, the basic elements of the field editor's duties. Officers assigned to headquarters between overseas tours normally serve as supervisors on the *Daily Report* or duty officers on the wire service.

FBIS officers assigned to overseas field bureaus supervise the collection and routing of monitored information. They must be managers, even on their first tours, as they direct the work of foreign national employees, who monitor, translate, and communicate the information obtained. Shift work performance is required, including evenings and weekends, but compensation is at premium rates. Overseas tours are usually for two years, and FBIS officers normally spend at least one-half of their careers abroad. They receive special housing and medical benefits and, in some cases, allowances.

The FBIS looks for new employees at the GS-07 through GS-10 levels depending on experience. Full performance level is generally at GS-11, while those who reach supervisory positions can expect to attain GS-12 and GS-13 status. A bachelor's degree is required. Majors in English, history, international relations, area studies, and print journalism are useful, as is experience in news writing and editing or teaching.

Resumés for employment with FBIS should be sent to Department A, Room 821, P.O. Box 1925, Washington, D.C. 20013.

Agricultural economic research positions are also available in the Directorate of Intelligence. The positions involve in-depth research and reporting on agricultural developments in foreign countries, including the USSR and China; international trade and international commodity markets for key agricultural products; and special topics involving worldwide food problems. Qualifications for employment include training in agricultural economics with a superior academic record, analytical ability, writing skill, and a research bent. Desirable, but of lesser importance, are area and language knowledge, advanced training in mathematics, and practical agricultural experience.

Applications for these agricultural economic research positions (with resumé, transcripts, and writing samples, such as term papers, a thesis, or a reprint of a professional paper) should be sent to Personnel Representative, Department A, Room 821-ER, P.O. Box 1925, Washington, D.C. 20013.

THE DIRECTORATE OF ADMINISTRATION—DDA

> *As a DDO officer I worked constantly, at Langley and abroad, with men and women from the DDA. They were business managers, concerned with budgets, finance, and payrolls. On occasion their experience and initiative were taxed, but they usually found a way to get the job done. Once I told a DDA officer that I needed, at once, a sizable supply of an exotic foreign currency in untraceable bills. "What denomination?" was his only question.*

The Office of Personnel Policy, Planning, and Management (OPPP&M) in the Directorate of Administration is responsible for developing CIA policies, standards, and procedures for personnel and staffing management. Specifically, those who work in OPPP&M guide and evaluate personnel management actions; authenticate, record, and report CIA position requirements and personnel transactions; operate a nationwide recruitment system; manage the employee benefits and services program; and provide management with human resources planning and analysis services. Newcomers to OPPP&M are given a short two- or three-week orientation followed by on-the-job training assignments and, in some cases, a formal training course.

The OPPP&M hires professional personnel officers usually in the GS-07 through GS-09 grade range, but some are employed above GS-09 based on their special qualifications and the openings within the OPPP&M. It develops personnel generalists capable of performing across-the-board duties. A four-year college degree is preferred with special consideration given to those holding degrees in public administration, business administration, personnel management, or psychology. Applicants with degrees in other fields are considered, if they have previous work experience in personnel, management, or related fields.

The Office of Finance (OF) is responsible for administering the financial operations of the CIA. The tasks include development and maintenance of accounting systems; establishment and supervision of financial regulations and procedures; performance of administrative, internal, and industrial audits; funding and disbursing, and payroll administration; and budget formulation and execution for CIA activities. Thus, the OF seeks recruits in the fields of accounting, contract auditing, internal auditing, and budgeting. Men and women with bachelor's and master's degrees in accounting, business administration, finance, commerce, or economics (with accounting experience) are favored. Starting salaries range from GS-07 through GS-09 depending on qualifications.

OF employees must be willing to serve overseas during their careers, and they are able to apply for, as the CIA states in its recruiting literature, "an interesting variety of work assignments." What is meant is that OF people are frequently assigned overseas, undercover, to CIA offices.

The Office of Security (OS) develops, maintains, and operates a comprehensive worldwide security program to protect CIA personnel, facilities, information, and activities. OS candidates should have an undergraduate degree, preferably in the social sciences. Entry levels are GS-07 through GS-09 depending on education and experience. Security officers are, for the most part, hired as generalists rather than specialists. An intellectual cop is a good description of a top-notch CIA security officer.

The OS requires its employees to be willing to serve abroad and throughout the United States and to accept different types of security assignments. The capacity to develop and report investigative details accurately is a prerequisite for a successful career.

Security officers are trained through a system of rotating assignments that guarantee exposure to a number of security-related functions. Career development can include training and assignment in such areas as employee background investigations, polygraph examinations, the processing of employee clearances, liaison, personnel protection, and physical security activities. Those with specialized training and experience in engineering fields find opportunities in such esoteric areas as computer security, among others.

The Office of Medical Services (OMS) is also a part of the Directorate of Administration and is responsible for planning and directing the CIA's medical program. Services include a medical selection program for CIA applicants; medical examinations and immunizations for employees and dependents going overseas; clinical services, preventive medicine, health education, and emergency health care; advisory assistance in support of medical intelligence production; and a psychiatric program including diagnostic and preventive psychiatry, psychiatric selection criteria, and psychiatric expertise in support of intelligence production.

Medical support by the OMS to CIA components includes medical training, health assessments, external liaison, and direction and support of the overseas medical program, including overseeing the activities of all medical personnel assigned outside the Washington, D.C., area.

Resident medical officers serve overseas and are responsible for providing medical care, advice, guidance, and support to employees and their dependents around the world. Starting salaries range from GSM-13 through GSM-15 (Government Schedule Medical; for medical doctors), depending on qualifications. Physicians who begin work for the CIA are eligible for an annual $7,000 to $10,000 bonus and are covered by malpractice insurance for line-of-duty medical practice.

Psychologists hired by the CIA usually work in one of the following fields: the Psychological Assessment Program, which selects the best candidates for CIA employment; counseling services, which assists employees in making career decisions; job performance research, which identifies psychological attributes needed to perform successfully in CIA assignments; human factors research, which, despite the name, designs and procures highly specialized equipment which can be operated easily and efficiently; and organizational consulting services, which provides managers with the techniques necessary to study and evaluate effectiveness of the CIA as an organization. Starting salary of a CIA psychologist is usually GS-12 or GS-13. A Ph.D. or the equivalent in the fields of clinical, research, industrial, counseling, or personnel management psychology is required.

Medical services officers are paramedics. Their duties include, but are not limited to, all phases of physical examination laboratory screening; attending to the diagnosis and treatment of chronic illnesses and medical emergencies; conducting training in survival skills, field medicine, cardiopulmonary resuscitation (CPR), and first-aid; establishing and operating independent duty dispensaries; and conducting health surveys. Starting salary for a CIA paramedic is customarily GS-06 or GS-07 depending on training and experience. Advancement to senior administrative or managerial positions is possible. A B.S. degree as a physician's assistant or medical technologist, associate degree in a medically related field, or equivalent military or civilian training is required.

The Office of Communications (OC) recruits young people known in CIA parlance as communicators. They install and maintain communications equipment, including transmitters and receivers ranging from high frequency to microwave, and install and operate high-speed data transmission equipment.

CIA communications employees generally start at GS-07 or GS-08. An associate degree in electronic technology or equivalent technical training is required. Knowledge of basic electronic theory, including basic logic and solid state, is needed, and military experience as electronic technician or civilian experience with a commercial electronics firm is preferred. OC employees must be willing to serve overseas and must be prepared for long hours of hard work during crisis periods.

THE DIRECTORATE OF SCIENCE AND TECHNOLOGY—DDS&T

When I became sufficiently senior to dine at the CIA's executive dining room, I enjoyed the opportunity to exchange war stories with my DDO colleagues and to visit with DDI and DDA administrators.

There was one small group who chatted with us about mundane matters, but never about what they were doing. They were the scientists and engineers from DDS&T. (Later, in newspaper revelations, we read of their endeavors: exploration ships, technical breakthroughs, high-altitude spy planes. . . .)

Of the four directorates that compose the CIA, the least known is the Directorate of Science and Technology (DDS&T). The information provided by the human agent, or spy, is vital to the intelligence process, but it is only one of several sources essential to adequate national intelligence. Photography and signals intelligence, which are collected by what are referred to as technical collection means or black boxes, have become ever more prominent sources of information. It is in the development of these technical means of collection and in the processing of the resulting information that DDS&T has accomplished impressive objectives through innovative application of state-of-the-art technology. The DDS&T supports photographic, electronic, and human means of collection through its staff which is expert in scientific disciplines such as digital data systems, space technology, microminiature electronic circuitry, and advanced battery technology.

If this description of DDS&T performance sounds fuzzy, it is because most of the work of the directorate is highly classified, and the imprecise terminology is intentional.

DDS&T is interested in applicants who have graduate or undergraduate degrees in the scientific and technological fields: electronic and mechanical engineering, physics, computer science, and operations research. A limited number of positions are filled by persons with degrees in foreign languages, journalism, political science, history, international relations, and geography. Specifically, job categories include electronic, mechanical, and optical engineering, photo science and technology, photogrammetry, computer science and programming, econometrics, behavioral and political science, chemistry, physics, art/illustration, editing, library science, and foreign languages.

Starting salaries range from GS-07 through GS-15.

THE DIRECTORATE OF OPERATIONS—DDO

The fourth directorate is the one that conducts the CIA's clandestine operations. Since so much has been written about this directorate, both accurately and inaccurately, it will be treated separately in Chapter IV.

OPPORTUNITIES FOR FOREIGN LANGUAGE SPECIALISTS

Foreign language specialists are employed by the CIA in three categories. The first, foreign literature analysis, is conducted by those who can combine foreign language skills with the subjects of foreign affairs, international economic relations, and science and technology. Responsibilities include reviewing foreign publications and reporting on current developments. These officers work with approximately sixty languages. They monitor publications ranging from newspapers to scholarly literature. Foreign language experts are usually assigned responsibility for an individual country, groups of countries, or specialized topics within a country, and coordinate their work with analysts throughout the U.S. government who are concerned with foreign affairs. Limited opportunities for overseas service are available.

The second category is the teaching of foreign languages. Foreign language teachers are hired by the CIA for its language school on a part-time, full-time, or intermittent basis. They must have teaching experience, and have native or near-native fluency. They teach small classes of well-educated people up to seven hours a day. CIA teachers are encouraged to attend professional conferences and to improve language skills through advanced study. Opportunities exist for research into problems of foreign language teaching and testing.

CIA language instructors are expected to have high to native competence in Russian, central Asian, eastern European, Middle Eastern, or Oriental languages. Those who teach the Germanic or Romance languages should have fluency in at least two of them.

U.S. citizenship is required. Salaries begin at GS-07 to GS-11, but can go higher depending on qualifications and openings available. To apply, send a resumé to:

Department A, Room 821
P.O. Box 1925
Washington, D.C. 20013

CIA translators, the third type of language specialist, work for a facility known as the U.S. Joint Publications Research Service (JPRS), which, as its name implies, provides translation services not only to the CIA but to various other government departments and agencies. The unit specializes in translation—again, in approximately sixty languages—in the social science, technical, and scientific fields.

The JPRS hires translators on a contract basis at a rate commensurate with educational background, experience, and test ratings after a language examination. Translators work at home, and all aspects of JPRS work can be conducted by mail. U.S. citizenship is not required.

The JPRS recently listed the languages where the current need for translators is greatest: Albanian, Arabic, Bulgarian, Chinese, Dutch/ Afrikaans, Greek, Hungarian, Japanese, Korean, Persian/Dari, Polish,

Russian (scientific disciplines only), Serbo-Croatian, Soviet central Asian, and Turkish.

Those interested in employment by correspondence as CIA translators should send a resumé of language(s), education, field of specialization, and experience to:

U.S. Joint Publications Research Service
1000 North Glebe Road
Arlington, Virginia 22201

CLERICAL CAREERS IN THE CIA

The CIA employs typists and stenographers for service in the Washington, D.C., area. Cost of travel and shipment of household effects for those hired who live more than fifty miles from CIA headquarters is reimbursed.

Minimum qualifications for those hired at the GS-04 to GS-06 levels specify that the employee be at least 17½ years of age, be a high school graduate or have a G.E.D., be a U.S. citizen (a spouse must also be a U.S. citizen), type forty words per minute, and take dictation at a rate of eighty words per minute.

After a period of service in the Washington, D.C., area, those secretaries and stenographers who are at least twenty-one years of age may apply for international assignments. In overseas posts additional compensation and various benefits are provided.

To apply, send resumé to:

Office of Personnel
Department A, Room 821
P.O. Box 1925
Washington, D.C. 20013

Or apply in person at 12:15 p.m. Monday through Friday:

Washington Area Recruitment Office
1820 North Fort Myer Drive
Rosslyn, Virginia (at the Rosslyn subway station)

SUMMER INTERNS IN FOREIGN STUDIES

A limited number of graduate students, or students just completing a B.A. degree who plan to enter graduate school, are accepted each summer at the CIA as interns. The program is for area specialists in China, Southeast Asia, Latin America, Africa, the Middle East, or Russia; also, students who intend to develop expertise in the areas of economics, geography, political science, history, linguistics, or international affairs. Interested students should send a short resumé form by December 15 expressing a desire to participate in the Summer Intern Program (these resumés are handled by an office separate from the regular employment section). Because of the time needed for a background investigation, receipt of the resumés before December 15 is essential.

IV
The Secret CIA

Those who seek challenging assignments overseas and, once in a while, James Bond adventures, will find the action in the CIA's Directorate of Operations (DDO). The men and women who work in the DDO refer to themselves as intelligence officers or case officers. The people who gather information and run operations for them, usually foreigners, are known as agents. Case officers and agents are usually described by journalists as spies, a term seldom used in the in-house CIA lexicon. The DDO is also known as the Clandestine Service.

In earlier years there has been a popular notion that the Clandestine Service was a public service refuge for the scions of the East Coast, Ivy League establishment. This was never true, even when the CIA was formed by a cadre of OSS veterans. A composite of the average CIA officer in secret operations shows that he (or she) is about thirty-three years of age, married, with two children. He holds a degree from a state university, speaks at least one foreign language, and has worked in at least two foreign countries. Abroad he often performs two functions, his cover duty and, when that day ends, his clandestine job. He claims no pay for overtime (and doesn't even when working at Langley) and contributes more time to the job than the ordinary nine-to-five worker. In his cover role, if he works in an embassy or one of the consulates, he always ranks below his peers in the Department of State and other agencies, but he recognizes that arrangement as absolutely necessary for him to operate.

Clandestine work in secret operations is not always exciting. Sometimes a CIA operative is like the military officer stationed on a bleak Aleutian Island, responsible for spotting Soviet missiles speeding toward a U.S. target. The assignment is vital but dull. Much intelligence work involves the acquisition of bits and pieces of information, and their storage in a manner which allows immediate retrieval. It is often a tedious business.

But, clandestine operations can also be exciting, and the practitioner is justified in perceiving himself as one of Smiley's people.

The case officer. In the CIA's Clandestine Service, success or failure of an intelligence endeavor depends on the case officer. He or she might be a specialist in a particular field such as Soviet operations. More often, the case officer is a generalist, sometimes known as a "street man," who can perform a variety of tasks. Principal among them is the hiring and firing of foreign nationals as information sources. In some regions abroad the work of the case officer is often risky and sometimes dangerous. More than thirty stars engraved in a marble wall at CIA headquarters commemorate officers killed in the line of duty; many of the stars are not identified by name, as the circumstances of death must remain secret.

During obligatory tours at headquarters the case officer works in a geographical division which supports overseas operations. The work of the case officer, at home and abroad, is always demanding, and calls for meticulous tradecraft, an adherence to strict rules of professional conduct so that mistakes in running an operation do not jeopardize the success or security of the endeavor.

Generally, case officers are recruited from among college graduates. Applicants who aspire to be DDO case officers are often anxious to begin their work in dark alleys abroad, but they must be patient and go back to school. Case officers usually enter CIA service through what is known as the Career Training Service; the neophytes are known in the CIA as CTs. The CT training program is conducted at a bucolic establishment much like a college campus. The instructors are case officers on home tours, and visiting lecturers from Langley give highly classified lectures about their experiences in espionage and covert action. Few students complain that they are bored.

The reports officer is the Clandestine Service specialist who forms a mosaic out of bits and pieces of information. All available information on a given subject or event is processed by the reports officer and then put into final form for transmission to intelligence customers abroad and in the United States. A CIA station complement usually includes one or more reports officers; at very small stations, case officers write their own reports.

Analysts and researchers maintain intelligence banks of information, based on current reporting by agents and case officers. Some work is in major DDO installations abroad, but most work is in area divisions at CIA headquarters.

The deep-cover officer. The trickiest assignment for a DDO officer overseas is when he or she uses nonofficial or deep cover. CIA people under official cover have a built-in margin for error. If a tradecraft mistake or bad luck compromises them with the local government, these officers are protected by official passports which means that, at worst, they will be declared *persona non grata* and sent home. (In 1971 the British government, exasperated by the high level of espionage by Soviet diplomats, expelled 107 of them at the same time!)

The deep-cover officer has no official protection. If he gets into trouble, he may be subject to prosecution under local laws. He cannot expect his own government to come to his defense, as a *démarche* from the U.S. embassy might only confirm that the American is, in fact, an intelligence operative.

Most DDO officers, at home and abroad, and under whatever cover, must lead double lives to be effective in their work and, in some cases, in order to survive. The problem is compounded in the case of the deep-cover officer. His tour abroad might stretch out for many years in the same country. He and his family must be prepared for a lonely, silent mission, where success is known only to a few colleagues. Deep cover operatives and their families have a tough and vital job to handle. Only the hardy should apply.

DDO managers are former case officers. Having demonstrated a flair for management, they become senior officers of the CIA as chiefs of station in the field and as branch and division chiefs at headquarters.

What case officers actually do is difficult to describe because the demands and situations they face overseas are so diverse that it would take another book to explain case officer responsibilities adequately. What follows are three examples that illustrate some of the things a case officer must do in the performance of his job; these three incidents actually happened in Latin America.

1. At a CIA station, it was decided to "intercept" a meeting between a Soviet KGB officer from the local embassy and an indigenous KGB agent. That is, knowing of the planned encounter, a CIA officer was to pose as a Soviet in order to learn more about the relationship between the Soviet embassy and the local agent and his political party. A case officer, exploiting his ability to speak Russian, met the agent on the pretext that the regular KGB case officer was ill, and that he was taking his place on an emergency basis. To add authenticity to the scenario, another CIA officer who also spoke Russian sat behind the wheel of a black automobile similar to one used by the Soviets—the ubiquitous Russian chauffeur. There

was an exchange of money and then a forty-five minute conversation. When the meeting ended the Latin American agent said to the CIA officer, "You know, I've been working for the KGB for six years, and you are the most professional KGB officer I've ever met!"

2. Two weeks later in another country it was necessary for a four-person team to conduct a surreptitious entry—an illegal break-in—in an effort to obtain vital, high-priority intelligence data from the offices of a hostile power. One member of this team was a woman. The team used the cover of electricians making repairs. Since there are no female electricians in Latin America, the CIA woman was disguised as a man, complete with a phony mustache.

3. An international conference was about to convene. Knowing the positions to be taken by countries not completely friendly to the United States was an intelligence requirement with obvious benefits for American negotiators at the conference. In one Latin American country, the CIA station obtained a photostatic copy of that country's position, but it was a lengthy document and there was no time to translate and cable it to the site of the meeting, thousands of miles away. The station chief summoned his most junior case officer and instructed him to board the next international flight, hand-carrying the vital piece of intelligence. On the plane the young officer kept touching the breast pocket of his coat, where he carried the purloined document. He had reason to be nervous. Directly across the aisle, close enough so that the CIA officer could have leaned across and touched him, was the foreign minister of the country in which he was stationed, also flying to the conference. The foreign minister spent the flight thumbing through *his* copy of the position paper!

The three episodes provide food for thought to those who consider a career in the DDO. The first involves deception and guile. The second and third—breaking and entering and theft of state secrets—are by normal standards criminal acts. *Espionage and covert action are illegal everywhere in the world.*

While an applicant for the Clandestine Service of the CIA ponders the questions of morality and personal ethics which he must face during his career, the issue of clandestine action operations should be addressed. Should the United States maintain clandestine activities at all? Despite the avalanche of words published and broadcast on the subject, few outside of the DDO, including many in the other services of the CIA, really understand what they might be abolishing—in short, what clandestine operations are and (equally important) what they are not, their limitations, and why they exist.

A discussion about covert operations must begin with a definition of what the Clandestine Service of the CIA does. It basically does two things: collects intelligence needed by policymakers to formulate policy and undertakes programs to assist policymakers in carrying out a policy. The first is known as espionage and the second covert action. Espionage seeks information important to the U.S. government which some foreign entity wishes to keep secret. Covert action endeavors to persuade a foreign entity to take action or to refrain from an action; circumstances and the nature of the persuasion preclude the attribution of covert action to the government. Propaganda in its many shades of gray (that is, degrees of concealment of sponsorship) may accomplish a covert action objective. Secret agents dealing directly with individuals in a position of influence are more likely to do so.

Strictly speaking, paramilitary operations (e.g., supporting a secret army) should not be classified under covert action. They relate to covert action as war compares with diplomacy. Paramilitary endeavors belie sooner or later the one condition essential to covert action, secrecy, and flout the old maxim that one should not attempt to cover a hippopotamus with a handkerchief.

The funding of foreign political parties, however, should be considered a covert action even though it is difficult to maintain secrecy in such a passionate milieu. Usually the passage of money is arranged through a black bag operation (i.e., a secret, under-the-table operation).

CIA critics have contended that the U.S. government should not be ashamed to support democratic forces overseas and, therefore, should fund deserving political parties openly, if at all. Although refreshingly straightforward, this approach overlooks one reality: the beneficiaries of such aid would be the first to insist that it be given discreetly. It would be political suicide for them to accept foreign assistance, just as it would be for a party in this country to do so. On the other hand, I found in serving in eight countries abroad that handsome subsidies given by the Soviets to Communist opposition parties surreptitiously are accepted as a fact of life by nearly all concerned, including most governments and peoples of the countries involved.

Clandestine operations have been condemned as immoral in principle and illegal in practice. This attitude naively sidesteps the problems of existing and, indeed, surviving in a world whose history continues to be determined by nations promoting their own interests at the expense of others, the League of Nations, United Nations, and similar laudable endeavors notwithstanding. More to the point, it would have the United States compete in the international arena blindfolded and with one hand tied behind its back. The grim state of world affairs is neither likely to improve much in our time nor, for that matter, in our children's or grandchildren's. Until it does, the nations of the world will continue to insist on their sovereign right to defend and advance their interests through clandestine operations, restricting any question of immorality or illegality to cases uncovered within their own national boundaries.

Whether the United States should conduct clandestine operations abroad is a subject worthy of debate. A discussion of the issues is usually reduced to the following terms:

1. If we consider it important to this country to have an *adequate* intelligence capability, we must recognize that resorting to clandestine means, including espionage specifically, is inevitable.

2. If we feel as a nation we can accept some clandestine means, such as espionage, but not others, such as covert action, at least our rationale should be clear.

3. If we decide that covert action is wrong because it constitutes meddling in other peoples' affairs, we should re-examine not only our intelligence activities but our entire foreign policy, our foreign aid program, and our tariff policies (to mention only a few examples) because each of these can have a profound effect on the internal affairs of any number of countries and very often is designed to have just such an effect.

My personal view is that our country must practice espionage as a vital adjunct to foreign policy. And I believe that in special situations the option of covert action should be open to American presidents.

Détente with the Soviet Union became a practical possibility when American intelligence developed the satellite capability to monitor Soviet adherence to arms and nuclear agreements. In America there are many perceptions of détente. Some view it with suspicion, some advocate it fervently. A majority of people concur that it is better than the disaster of a nuclear war. But the French word *détente*, when translated into Russian, means either "release the trigger tension" or "unload the gun." It does not mean discard or unload the gun and melt down the bullets, and until that interpretation changes, good intelligence is indispensable to the United States in a era of détente, and every indication is that it will continue to be so for generations.

But why covert action?

A former colleague often told the story of two Americans who visited the Moscow zoo. They were amazed to find a large bear and a small lamb in the same cage. They summoned the zookeeper. "This is amazing," the Americans said. "We have never seen a bear and a lamb in the same cage." "Oh, yes," the zookeeper replied. "This is to prove that co-existence is possible. This demonstrates that détente can work." The zookeeper looked about to be sure he was not being overheard. Then he added, "Of course, we have to change the lamb every day."

In the final analysis, someone has to look after the lambs of the world.*

If, after careful consideration, you still want to work in the CIA's DDO, these are the guidelines to follow when applying as a candidate for the agency's Career Training program: First, be prepared to be patient while a security check is being made on you and those close to you. CT applicants are normally accepted into the program in February, May, August, and November of each year. Your application should be submitted at least four to six months before the time you would like to go to work because of the obligatory delay in conducting the security investigation. If accepted, your starting grade will usually range from GS-08 to GS-11.

Second, be aware that the senior officers who will be reviewing your application (most of them veteran overseas case officers) will be looking for the following qualifications: a strong interest in international affairs; the ability to communicate orally and in writing; strong interpersonal skills (i.e., the ability to win friends and influence people); the ability to speak a foreign language or the aptitude to learn one or more; and although not required, but an advantage, overseas experience of one kind or another, such as travel, residence, or military service.

Third, prepare a resumé that discusses your specific qualifications. Include phone numbers (day and evening), college major, a concise statement explaining why you want to work for the CIA, and a brief description of your principal strengths. Come on fairly strong; modesty is not always a virtue in the makeup of a Clandestine Service operator.

Mail your resumé to:

Office of Personnel
Dept. A, Room 281
P.O. Box 1925
Washington, D.C. 20013

Do *not* include "Central Intelligence Agency" in the address. If you are going to spend an entire career working under cover, you might as well begin to learn tradecraft now. If your application attracts interest, you will be contacted for a confidential interview within a few weeks.

Before mailing a resumé, however, think about it again. The cloak-and-dagger side of the CIA is not a career for everyone. It is a career for

---

*Some of the preceding paragraphs are from my book *The Night Watch*, published by Atheneum and available in paperback from the Ballantine Espionage/Intelligence Library.

a very few special men and women with skills, self-discipline, self-reliance, and initiative. It is a career for those who welcome excitement in challenging situations that demand critical, on-the-spot decisions.

V
The Federal Bureau of Investigation

The FBI today has three primary targets: organized crime, white-collar crime, and foreign counterintelligence. Special agents monitor the activities of Soviet intelligence officers throughout the United States, as well as spies from the bloc countries, Cuba, and the more violence-prone countries of the Third World, such as Libya. The game of international intrigue is sophisticated, but it is played with hardball rules, and FBI officers must operate against seasoned KGB officers. Instances of FBI success in thwarting the schemes of foreign agents are often read about in daily newspapers; just as often the victory is a silent one.

The FBI does not recruit personnel specifically for intelligence assignments. Rather, special agents are assigned to the spy beat because of special qualifications or experience. Those who prefer the espionage-counterintelligence assignments can usually wangle a job in the intelligence sections of the FBI if they are prepared for the long hours and tedious assignments that come along with the occasional excitement of spy-counterspy games.

The important business of the FBI is carried out by special agents, the rough equivalent of the CIA's case officers. Those who are not special agents (typists, clerks, technicians) are known, sad to say, as nonagents.

Special agent candidates must be U.S. citizens, between twenty-three and thirty-five years of age, possess a valid driver's license, and be prepared to serve anywhere in the bureau's jurisdiction. (In addition to the fifty states, there are FBI offices in Puerto Rico and major world capitals.)

Physical requirements are strict. Special agent candidates must be in excellent physical condition with no defects that would interfere in firearms use, raids, or defensive tactics. Applicants must have uncorrected vision not less than 20/200 (Snellen) and corrected 20/20 in one eye and 20/40 in the other eye. All candidates must pass a color vision test. They must also meet specific hearing requirements in order to qualify to be special agents. Audiometer tests to detect any hearing deficiency are administered to all candidates.

After the physical examination, applicants may choose one of five entrance programs to become a special agent.

The Law Program is for resident law school graduates with two years of resident, undergraduate college work. (Resident means mail-order diplomas are not recognized.)

The Accounting Program requires a four-year resident college degree with a major in accounting.

The Language Program is for those who have a four-year resident degree from college plus fluency in one or more foreign languages (useful if an overseas assignment is desired).

The Modified Program accepts those who have a four-year resident college degree of any kind, plus three years' full-time work experience. If you have an advanced degree, the full-time work experience need be only two years.

The Science Program is for resident college degree candidates who have a bachelor's, master's, or doctoral degree in electrical engineering or metallurgy; or a master's or doctoral degree in physics, toxicology, mathematics, or engineering science; or a master's in business or public administration, computer science, computer systems, management information sciences or systems, or a comparable degree with major emphasis on analysis and development of business/financial information systems; or a bachelor's plus three years scientific professional experience in the major field or allied area: biological or engineering science, geology, pharmacy, or toxicology. Individuals with biological sciences degrees must have satisfactorily completed sixteen semester hours in chemistry (including organic chemistry) and eight semester hours in physics. Also acceptable is a bachelor's degree plus three years' experience as a systems or programmer analyst handling business/financial type systems or applications with a major in: business or public administration, management science or systems, computer science, or science with a computer science major or course concentration.

In addition, applicants who have expertise as firearms examiners, explosives examiners, document examiners, and fingerprint examiners may qualify under the Science Program. College transcripts and a detailed resumé showing experience in these areas will be necessary to determine if an applicant qualifies under these options.

Whatever the entrance program, special agent applicants undergo an initial battery of written examinations that are scored by computer at FBI headquarters in Washington. Should an applicant rank high enough as the result of the testing, he or she is afforded a formal interview, which is again computerized. The highest ranked individuals in each of the entrance programs are given consideration for employment based on the needs of the bureau and are thoroughly investigated for employment. A polygraph examination may also be requested.

Newly appointed special agents report to the nearest FBI field division office for oath of office and then proceed to the FBI Academy at Quantico, Virginia, where they undergo training for fifteen weeks. New special agents receive regular salary while in training. The schooling usually consists of classroom instruction, physical fitness, and firearms training.

School means tests, and the minimum passing grade on each academic examination is 85 percent, and disqualifying conditions will result in dismissal. These conditions are: failing any two exams; failing to achieve twenty-four points in the physical fitness program or failing to demonstrate proficiency in defensive tactics; not having a passing score on all qualifying firearms courses by the eleventh week of training; sloppy handling of weapons during training, regardless of score; failing to demonstrate proficiency in simulated arrest situations; or violating conduct rules and regulations during training.

Physical Fitness Tests and Rating Scale for FBI Special Agent Trainees

Men		Women	
Pull-Ups		Modified Pull-Ups	
Number Completed	Points	Number Completed	Points
1	1	3	1
2	2	6	2
3	3	9	3
4	4	12	4
5	5	15	5

		Men and women	
Push-Ups		Sit-Ups	
Number Completed	Points	Number Completed	Points
15	1	30	1
20	2	35	2
25	3	40	3
30	4	45	4
35	5	50	5

120-Yard Shuttle Run		Two-Mile Run	
Time	Points	Time	Points
29 sec. and over	1	18:31—19:00	5
27—28.9	2	18:01—18:30	6
25—26.9	3	17:31—18:00	7
22—24.9	4	17:01—17:30	8
Under 22 seconds	5	16:31—17:00	9
		16:30 and under	10

Total possible points	30
Qualifying score	24

WHERE TO APPLY

Application for employment in the FBI may be made in person at any of the field offices listed below. In addition, there are resident agencies in many other cities where you may apply. (The address of the nearest office is listed in the front of your telephone directory.)

Albany, New York
Albuquerque, New Mexico
Alexandria, Virginia
Anchorage, Alaska
Atlanta, Georgia
Baltimore, Maryland
Birmingham, Alabama
Boston, Massachusetts
Buffalo, New York
Butte, Montana
Charlotte, North Carolina
Chicago, Illinois
Cincinnati, Ohio
Cleveland, Ohio
Columbia, South Carolina
Dallas, Texas
Denver, Colorado
Detroit, Michigan
El Paso, Texas
Honolulu, Hawaii
Houston, Texas
Indianapolis, Indiana
Jackson, Mississippi
Jacksonville, Florida
Kansas City, Missouri
Knoxville, Tennessee
Las Vegas, Nevada
Little Rock, Arkansas
Los Angeles, California
Louisville, Kentucky

Memphis, Tennessee
Miami, Florida
Milwaukee, Wisconsin
Minneapolis, Minnesota
Mobile, Alabama
Newark, New Jersey
New Haven, Connecticut
New Orleans, Louisiana
New York, New York
Norfolk, Virginia
Oklahoma City, Oklahoma
Omaha, Nebraska
Philadelphia, Pennsylvania
Phoenix, Arizona
Pittsburgh, Pennsylvania
Portland, Oregon
Richmond, Virginia
Sacramento, California
St. Louis, Missouri
Salt Lake City, Utah
San Antonio, Texas
San Diego, California
San Francisco, California
San Juan, Puerto Rico
Savannah, Georgia
Seattle, Washington
Springfield, Illinois
Tampa, Florida
Washington, D.C.

Or you may request an application by writing to Director, Federal Bureau of Investigation, Washington, D.C. 20535.

VI
The National Security Agency

The most secret of all United States secret organizations is the National Security Agency (NSA). It is the federal government agency responsible for all United States communications security activities and for development of foreign intelligence information crucial to the nation's defense.

While it is no secret that the NSA is in the business of making and breaking codes, the work in this area is highly classified. But cryptography is only a part of the work performed by the NSA. The agency conducts a vast research and development program in the field of specialized communications equipment. Some of these projects have been so dramatic as to significantly advance the state of the art in the scientific and commercial world at large. Past breakthroughs originating in NSA laboratories have included the first large-scale computer, the first solid-state computer, and certain (read classified) applications of high-density storage technology.

Cryptography, the development of code and cipher systems, is the most unusual occupation found at the NSA. With the advent of new and increasingly sophisticated communications systems, the field of cryptography has grown dramatically over the years. Scientifically devised, tested, and selected cryptographic systems are used to ensure the maximum degree of security for the transmission of sensitive information. Since cryptography is seldom offered as a course of study in college, specialized training is provided at NSA in the classrooms of its own National Cryptologic School and in rotating project assignments.

The NSA was established in 1952 by presidential directive to be the national authority for all United States communications intelligence activities. The NSA headquarters building is at Fort George G. Meade, near Baltimore, Maryland, and not far from Washington, D.C. Some employees work overseas in tours of two to three years.

Because of the secret nature of its work, the NSA sets its own job definitions, conducts its own aptitude testing, and recruits its new employees directly. All applicants must be U.S. citizens. Professional and preprofessional employees are recruited from all over the country, especially from colleges and industry. Extensive pre-employment procedures include personal interviews, a background investigation, and a medical examination. For these reasons it is important that applicants contact the NSA at least six months before graduating from college or before leaving their present commercial position.

Some of the tasks performed by the NSA are:

1. Collection of signals intelligence information for national foreign intelligence purposes with guidance from the director of Central Intelligence;

2. Processing of signals intelligence information;

3. Dissemination of signals intelligence (foreign) to authorized elements of the government, including the military services;

4. Collection, processing, and dissemination of signals intelligence information for counterintelligence purposes;

5. Provision of signals intelligence support for the conduct of military operations;

6. Conduct of research and development;

7. Protection of the security of its activities, property, information, and employees;

8. Conduct of foreign cryptologic liaison relationships—for intelligence purposes conducted in accordance with policies formulated by the director of Central Intelligence. (Although it has constant liaison with the CIA, the NSA is an agency of the Department of Defense.)

Entry level employment opportunities usually exist at the NSA for graduates in: computer engineering, electronic engineering, systems engineering, and electronic engineering technology. Three broad engineering fields are open at NSA: research and development (R&D), communications systems, and electronic data systems. R&D engineers at NSA perform advanced laboratory assignments while maintaining close contact with outside industry. Projects are usually carried out by groups of two or three junior engineers working under the direction of a senior engineer. Laboratory work ranges from theoretical problem solving to the creation of prototype models of equipment used in providing secure communications capability, communications information recording, data processing, and computing.

Systems engineers at NSA are involved in all phases of a project. Entering at the initial design and development stage, they follow experimental equipment through fabrication, acceptance testing, and production of an acceptable model by the contractor. Systems engineers perform evaluative tasks relative to reliability, compatibility with existing systems, and environmental acceptability.

The data processing and computing center at NSA is one of the largest in the world. NSA engineers are quickly exposed to the most advanced equipment built by NSA and virtually every commercial producer. After an initial assignment in the newly hired engineer's field of interest, he or she is given subsequent projects systematically to increase technical breadth and responsibility for project management.

Computer science. NSA's computer complex contains commercially available equipment as well as numerous specially designed and built devices. NSA careers in the computing field provide mixtures of such disciplines and technologies as systems design, programming languages, operating systems, compilers, applications analysis and communications, and retrieval systems.

Mathematics. NSA mathematicians are assigned in three areas: consulting with analysts on current communications problems, providing technical assistance to the communications systems specialists, and conducting long-range research in computing and communications. Areas of particular interest are probability theory, statistics, Fourier analysis, modern algebra, Galois theory, matrix theory, and stochastic processes. Many mathematicians at the bachelor's degree level enter intensive training programs in data systems for intelligence operations (e.g., cryptanalysis, communications security, or communications traffic analysis).

Physics. NSA physicists study the development of new and innovative communications and information processing equipment, and apply them to technical problem areas. NSA physicists are involved in such R&D areas as semiconductor physics, superconductivity, surface physics, quantum electronics, solids, and electromagnetic propagation.

Physical science/liberal arts. Internships and on-the-job assignments are designed to facilitate the transition from campus to NSA's major career areas for bachelor's level physical science and liberal arts majors who successfully compete in NSA's Professional Qualifications Test. This exam is given annually in November at over one hundred locations nationwide. Successful applicants are trained in such fields as computer systems, cryptography, communications security, and signals research and analysis. New employees at NSA who desire to undertake advanced study find a unique opportunity when working at Fort Meade. Full-time sponsorship is available on a competitive basis under the NSA Fellowship Program. Successful candidates are paid full salary as well as tuition while they complete their graduate work. Those who wish to attend any of the nearby universities—which include such fine schools as Johns Hopkins University, the University of Maryland, Georgetown, American, Catholic, and Howard Universities—for part-time graduate work in a job-related field may do so with NSA tuition assistance. And, NSA scientists and engineers are encouraged to attend and to participate in conferences and symposia of professional organizations throughout the country.

Linguistics. NSA offers careers in many challenging areas, including highly specialized research fields, for those with a flair for foreign languages: translating technical materials into English; transcribing or "gisting" spoken materials; preparing studies in one or more foreign languages; or compiling linguistic aids such as glossaries, handbooks, or special products of language analysis. Other assignments could include preparing grammars or courses for poorly documented languages, teaching foreign languages, or working in peripheral fields such as computer applications to linguistic problems.

Also, NSA is interested in people with or without college degrees who are proficient in a Slavic, Middle Eastern, or Asian language.

Because it is restricted in the degree of information it can provide to applicants due to the highly classified nature of its mission, NSA stresses the cultural and recreational opportunities found in nearby Baltimore and Washington, D.C. It is true that few areas in the country offer a wider choice of after-office-hours enjoyment: museums and theaters, historical sites, fine restaurants, and championship professional football, baseball, and basketball teams.

Students interested in a career at NSA should check with their placement office to arrange an interview with the NSA representative visiting their campus. If an interview cannot be scheduled, they should write to the following address:

> Director, National Security Agency
> Attn: M32 (Recruitment)
> Fort George G. Meade, Maryland 20755

VII
The Defense Intelligence Agency

The Defense Intelligence Agency (DIA) is the senior, central component in the Department of Defense responsible for intelligence activities. It satisfies the foreign intelligence requirements of the Secretary of Defense, the Joint Chiefs of Staff, and the Unified and Specific Commands. It provides guidance to a number of Defense Department components connected with intelligence, and acts as a clearinghouse for their intelligence production.

DIA manages the Defense Attaché System, which assigns military attachés to U.S. embassies around the world. The soldier-diplomats conduct liaison with local military units, arrange for U.S. training in many countries, and collect order-of-battle information on foreign armies.

The director of the National Security Agency reports indirectly to the DIA through the Department of Defense, but the NSA is largely an autonomous institution. The various military intelligence services are directly responsible to the DIA. Each of the four services has its intelligence arm and each has its own intelligence requirements.

Army intelligence provides specialized intelligence support to the army worldwide. Responsibilities include the collection, production, and dissemination of military and military-related foreign intelligence, including information on indications and warning capabilities, plans, and weapons systems and equipment; the conduct of counterintelligence activities and dissemination of counterintelligence studies and reports; and the development, procurement, and management of tactical intelligence systems and equipment.

Naval intelligence works to fulfill the intelligence, counterintelligence, investigative, and security requirements and responsibilities of the Department of the Navy. It also provides highly specialized collection and analysis related to navy security concerns.

Air force intelligence conducts and manages collection, processing and analysis, and dissemination activities to meet worldwide air force and national intelligence needs. Among the military services, the air force has the largest intelligence program, and its Foreign Technology Division is a leading national source of analysis of foreign aircraft and missiles.

Marine corps intelligence focuses on providing responsive intelligence support to marine corps tactical commanders, primarily in the amphibious warfare mission area, but also across the full spectrum of marine corps worldwide contingency concerns. Marine corps intelligence works closely with naval intelligence, both at the national and fleet levels.

THE DEFENSE ATTACHÉ SYSTEM

The senior military officer assigned to an American embassy abroad is known as the defense attaché. In all but the smallest embassies the defense attaché—who might be from any of the services; the position often rotates between the services—has a staff that includes an army, navy, air force, and marine attaché. In very large and important foreign capitals the defense attaché's responsibilities are extensive, and his staff quite large. (In Washington, D.C., for instance, Britain's defense attaché presides over a staff of eight military aides and more than one hundred civilians.)

Defense attachés are military diplomats, sometimes described as overt spies, who are charged with finding out as much as they can about their host country's military establishment without engaging in clandestine or illegal activities. As one senior Department of State officer described the function, "Military attachés give military advice to their ambassadors; they promote arms sales and the exchange of people; but they do all these things to get additional entree for intelligence sharing, even if it's in-house gossip like who are the rising stars in the Pentagon, who makes the decisions. . . ."

Military historian Alan Gropman of the National War College is even more direct: "An attaché is really a spy, whether he is on your side or not."

Attachés, no matter what nation they represent, like to downplay their espionage role, preferring such terms as *observers* and *liaison officers*. It is true that in many situations their activities are largely overt, but nearly always during wartime and frequently in peacetime military attachés engage in cloak-and-dagger espionage. The Soviet Union, for instance, traditionally uses attaché cover for agents of its military intelligence service, known as the GRU. (In 1982 the senior military attaché of the Soviet embassy in Washington was expelled after FBI agents apprehended him in the act of attempting to buy classified U.S. documents.)

U.S. military attachés abroad are senior officers from one of the four services. And the chief of the DIA and his principal deputy are invariably military personnel, as are the majority of DIA employees. Thus, those who aspire to a career in military intelligence can seek it within the framework of regular military service and can apply at the nearest army, navy, air force, or marine corps recruiting office or should enroll in college Reserve Officers Training Corps (ROTC) programs.

The most profitable path to a career in military intelligence, however, is followed after graduation from one of the service academies. In order to obtain such cost-free education it is certainly useful to be from a military family or to have a friend in a high place. But it is not true that all young people entering service academies have special connections with government or service officials. The most common route is by nomination of a senator or representative, and most of them welcome applications from any constituent, whatever his or her family connections.

Applications can also be made through the vice president of the United States. Enlisted military personnel or members of ROTC may apply via their branches of the armed forces. Candidates are expected to be between seventeen and twenty-one years of age, highly ranked in high school or college grades, in excellent physical condition, and contemplating a long-term military career.

For information, write to:

U.S. Air Force Academy/RRV
Colorado Springs, Colorado 80840

Director of Admissions
U.S. Military Academy
West Point, New York 10996

Superintendent
U.S. Naval Academy (Candidate Guidance)
Annapolis, Maryland 21402

DIA CAREERS WITHOUT UNIFORMS

The DIA is not exclusively a military agency, many of its officers, analysts, and employees being civilian. A recent advertisement in the *Washington Post* read: "Jobs. Army Intelligence in Arlington, Virginia, has openings for engineers, illustrators and intelligence specialists, Grades GS-07 through GS-12." Many DIA civilian officers are in senior positions (GS-15 through GS-16) and spend their entire careers working in the Pentagon.

The DIA describes its nonmilitary people as part of "a civilian team engaged in collecting, analyzing, evaluating, interpreting and disseminating information which affects our national security."

Those interested in a civilian career with the DIA should send a resumé or Standard Form 171 to:

Defense Intelligence Agency
Civilian Personnel Operations
Division (Dept. CL)
Washington, D.C. 20301

THE DEFENSE INTELLIGENCE COLLEGE

Originally called the Defense Intelligence School, this unusual training academy was founded in Washington, D.C., in 1962 to educate military personnel and civilians to perform in the intelligence community. The name was changed in 1983 to recognize the fact that the school had become a true college—the only one in the U.S. that offers a master's degree in intelligence.

The Department of Defense directive which provides the charter for the school's operation describes the college as "a professional educational and research institution under the direction of the Director, Defense Intelligence Agency," and identifies its mission "to provide education and training to meet the requirements of the defense community in strategic intelligence areas. This mission requires the College to identify, conduct and evaluate the academic and professional educational requirements necessary to satisfy the stated needs of its users." The users of the Defense Intelligence College are students from the four military services, the NSA, CIA, FBI, and other government agencies.

In carrying out its mission, the college is involved in four specific educational activities. There are educational programs at the bachelor's and master's degree level, professional programs and courses, training to prepare personnel for duty in the defense attaché system, and academic research on topics of significance to present and future intelligence missions. A master's degree in the strategic intelligence program is designed to enable selected military officers and civilians to enhance their preparation for important command, staff, and policymaking positions.

In addition to its full-time teaching staff, the Defense Intelligence College invites prominent members of the military, the government, and the private sector to serve as guest lecturers, adjunct professors, and advisors for research. More than 16,000 military and civilian personnel have graduated from the college, and the annual enrollment is now in excess of 2,000 students.

VIII
The Department of the Treasury

One of the larger organizations in the U.S. federal government is the Department of the Treasury. It has many responsibilities beyond the printing of the currency and the minting of the coins we use—one being to retrieve some of our money through the Internal Revenue Service.

Three departments in the Treasury must conduct intelligence operations in order to perform their missions: the Secret Service, the U.S. Customs Service, and the Bureau of Alcohol, Tobacco, and Firearms. The primary mission of these organizations is enforcement. But the successful prosecution of violators and the protection of the president and his high-level aides require some cloak-and-dagger work that must be performed by undercover operatives.

Those who seek careers in intelligence in its classic mold—espionage, analysis, covert action—will want to apply to the CIA, NSA, DIA, or the FBI; in the latter case with the expectation of assignment to the bureau's counterintelligence element. But would-be intelligence officers may also wish to consider employment in the Department of the Treasury to support enforcement activities.

THE SECRET SERVICE

Shortly after the assassination attempt on President Reagan's life in 1981, Secret Service director H. Stuart Knight was questioned by a congressional committee. He was asked how he would use extra funds if his budget for protecting the president were to be doubled. "My response would be," Knight replied, "in some way, to try and enhance our intelligence capability."

The primary task of the Secret Service is to protect the president and other notables. The name of the agency, which is a part of the Department of the Treasury, conjures up images of men jogging beside the presidential

53

limousine; or of steely eyed agents watching the hands of people straining to shake hands with the president; or, more vividly, of a Secret Service agent turning into the line of fire of an assassin's bullet, using his body as a shield to protect the president. These graphic recollections tend to make us forget other Secret Service responsibilities. Among them are the collection of information, investigation, and law enforcement duties against counterfeiting and forgery.

When the Secret Service was established in 1865, it had no responsibility for protecting chief executives (despite the fact that authority to form the Secret Service was given by President Lincoln on the day he was assassinated). The mission of the first ten-man Secret Service unit was to combat widespread currency counterfeiting, when over 1,600 private banks printed their own currency. It was not until 1906 that Congress authorized the Secret Service to protect the president—after Presidents Garfield and McKinley had been slain by assassins in 1881 and 1901, respectively. Since that time, ensuring the security of the White House and its occupants and certain other persons has been the top priority. But, in addition to detecting and apprehending counterfeiters and forgers, the Secret Service is often given ad hoc assignments. Agents guarded the Mona Lisa when the painting was exhibited in the United States and provided security for His Holiness the Pope during an American tour. And, during the Spanish-American War and World War II, the Secret Service conducted some U.S. counterespionage programs.

Secret Service agents perform the following tasks:

1. Protect the president and vice president and their immediate families; former presidents and their wives; the widow of a former president until she dies or remarries; minor children of a former president until they are sixteen years old; major presidential and vice presidential candidates and, if they are elected, protect them before they assume office; and visiting heads of state. The president can request, and often does, that the Secret Service watch out for other dignitaries when they travel abroad.

2. Detect and arrest offenders for counterfeiting coins, currency, stamps, and other U.S. securities.

3. Suppress the forgery and fraudulent negotiation of government checks, bonds, and other securities.

4. Investigate criminal violations of the Federal Deposit Insurance Act, the Federal Land Bank Act, and the Government Losses in Shipment Act.

Special agent applicants for the Secret Service must have a college degree in any field or the equivalent in education and work experience. He or she must be under thirty-five years of age and be in excellent physical shape. Vision must be 20/20 in one eye and at least 20/40 in the other.

An agent is expected to become adept at judo, karate, the use of weapons, bomb detection, high-speed pursuit, and defensive driving (learning how to smash a car through a roadblock, for instance). Recruits are trained for four months at one of two Secret Service academies, at Brunswick, Georgia, or Beltsville, Maryland. The curriculum includes investigative techniques. Students are taught to work in teams, each being aware of the other's capabilities in an emergency.

When screening candidates, Secret Service recruiters attempt to identify people who can deal with other people, work under pressure, and make on-the-spot decisions during a crisis. They look for previous work experience as a manager in civilian life or as an officer in the military. Few Secret Service agents are former policemen because those young enough to qualify lack supervisory or investigative experience. "An agent must be honest and experienced, must be mature," comments one special agent. But, he adds, "Not too old to run beside the president's car."

Only a minority of Secret Service agents, in fact, run alongside VIP limousines. The great majority of 1,500 agents are stationed in one hundred Secret Service field offices around the United States, in Puerto Rico, and in Paris. Some of their time is spent preparing for the time when one of the notables the Secret Service protects (known as protectees) might be visiting. Most of the work day, however, is devoted to investigative tasks—such as checking out one of the more than 14,000 reports received each year from private citizens about persons they believe to be a threat to the president's life. About 400 of these cases are sufficiently serious to call for the arrest of the person being investigated.

The Office of Protective Intelligence (OPI) in Washington is where Secret Service agents are intelligence officers in the fullest sense of the word. The number of suspect individuals and groups of which the OPI must keep abreast has accumulated over the years to about 40,000. Some 350 of them are considered to be extremely dangerous, and every effort is made to keep them on the Secret Service radar screen. Computers are used extensively for this reason.

The OPI is responsible for collecting, evaluating, and storing protective security data. It conducts liaison with other agencies, especially the FBI, CIA, and Immigration and Naturalization Service. The OPI is also responsible for maintaining a safe environment for the president and other dignitaries, ranging from physical safety (hotel security) to sweeping the suite, ensuring no electronic devices exist in the rooms.

Secret Service agents in the OPI and in field stations pass intelligence they acquire to their colleagues who actually guard the president. Agents must be prepared to blend into many informal situations, such as the agents who accompanied Presidents Eisenhower and Ford on the golf course with machine guns stowed in golf bags. Agents usually wear conservative business suits and always wear a lapel pin that identifies them as agents on duty. Or, a Secret Service special agent may have to attend a very formal social function, such as a state dinner at the White House. The Secret Service does not supply the evening clothes, but these costs are tax deductible.

Secret Service special agents enter on duty at ratings of GS-06 to GS-08. Applicants should write to:

United States Secret Service
Personnel Division
1800 G Street, NW
Washington, D.C. 20223

The Secret Service supervises the United States Secret Service Uniformed Division. Its members perform police-like guard assignments to protect the president and vice president, their families and residences, and any building in which presidential offices are located. They also guard the scores of foreign diplomatic establishments in Washington using patrols, fixed posts, and canine teams.

Requirements for the Uniformed Division are:

1. U.S. citizenship.
2. Vision of at least 20/40 in each eye, correctable to 20/20.
3. Weight in proportion to height.
4. Passing a physical exam, which is free at the Washington, D.C., Police and Fire Clinic.
5. A high school diploma or equivalent or one year experience as a police officer in a city over 500,000 population.
6. Passing a written test and a personal interview.
7. Qualifying for a top secret clearance.
8. Having a valid driver's license.
9. Being willing to work shifts and weekends.

THE U.S. CUSTOMS SERVICE

The U.S. Customs Service, a part of the Department of the Treasury, was one of the first agencies established in the United States when, in 1789, the First Congress directed it to assess and collect the revenue on imported merchandise and to enforce customs and related laws.

Today, customs enforces its own laws and regulations as well as those for more than three dozen other federal agencies. It conducts a variety of antismuggling and other law enforcement programs connected with international trade and travel; processes people and merchandise coming into the United States; collects duties and taxes; protects government revenue against fraud and theft; and keeps items harmful to our welfare (such as illicit and dangerous drugs) from entering the United States. The Customs Service employs about 14,000 persons throughout the nation, Puerto Rico, and the U.S. Virgin Islands at the nearly three hundred ports of entry along U.S. land and sea borders. Selected officers are assigned to overseas posts.

The enforcement responsibilities of customs require some undercover operations involving intelligence expertise on the part of customs agents. Most of this activity is carried out by special agents.

Special agents of customs engage in a variety of investigations ranging from criminal fraud against the revenue to all manner of smuggling violations, neutrality and currency cases, and major cargo thefts. Special agents are trained in modern investigative and law enforcement techniques, such as the use of firearms, undercover operations, surveillance techniques, rules of evidence, and courtroom demeanor. Most of the officers involved in this aspect are assigned to duty stations throughout the United States at ports of air and sea entry; frequent travel is involved in the course of surveillance work.

To qualify as a special agent of customs, an applicant must:

1. Be a U.S. citizen who has not reached his or her thirty-fifth birthday.

2. Successfully complete an oral interview and personal background investigation.

3. Establish an eligibility rating on the Treasury Enforcement Agent Examination (TEA), a test to measure investigative aptitude. Entrance level appointments from the TEA register are made at grades GS-05 and GS-07. Applicants with specialized law enforcement experience or education should establish eligibility on the mid-level register for appointment at grades GS-09 through GS-12.

4. Have at least one year of progressively responsible experience that demonstrates skill in dealing effectively with people. Also needed is no less than two years of specialized criminal investigative or comparable experience which calls for tact, judgment, and resourcefulness, plus the ability to analyze and evaluate evidence.

5. Be in excellent physical condition with good muscular development. You need distant vision of at least 20/40 in one eye and 20/100 in the other without glasses, correctable to at least 20/20 in one eye and 20/30 in the other with glasses; good near vision, color, and depth perception; and, reads Customs Service recruitment literature, "Persons with a hearing aid, noticeable deformities or disfiguring conditions should not apply."

58

Note: One scholastic year of education above high school is equivalent to nine months of work experience. A bachelor's degree is fully qualifying for appointment at the GS-05 level.

CUSTOMS SERVICE INTELLIGENCE OPERATIONS

Investigative and undercover work by customs personnel is conducted as a necessary adjunct in enforcement activities. In the classical sense, intelligence operations are carried out by professionals in the Washington headquarters intelligence division. The experts in that unit are concerned with strategic intelligence—the long-range interpretive analysis of trends and geographical areas of interest to customs, such as the production of narcotics in a foreign country, which may eventually become contraband with a U.S. destination. Many of the officers in the division are professionals who develop their expertise in other government agencies; some are customs enforcement personnel who serve rotational tours.

In each of its regional offices, the Customs Service maintains a tactical intelligence unit, devoted to day-by-day support to enforcement operations. The officers involved in intelligence work in these units are usually customs career people.

Wherever intelligence functions are performed in customs, the personnel are recruited from other agencies or become involved during routine customs activities. Thus, applicants with interest in intelligence work should not apply with that area of employment in mind. Rather, they should seek jobs in the Customs Service in a traditional position and await an opportunity to move into intelligence work.

When customs finds itself conducting secret operations, it is sometimes, as it is said in the trade, sexy. The following, for example, are the opening paragraphs of a *New York Times* story (October 4, 1981, page 1) about a Customs Service endeavor in New York in 1981:

> A cache of antique books stolen in London was recovered and a Columbia University graduate student was arrested by customs agents who enlisted a New York rare-book seller for an undercover drama played out over lunch Friday at the Princeton Club.
>
> Wearing a bulletproof vest, the bookseller exchanged $11,000 in cash for four of the 267 missing volumes, including a 1683 edition of Galileo's "Discorsi." When the lunch ended, agents waiting outside seized the suspect and they later recovered a score of the other missing books at the suspect's Riverside Drive apartment, authorities said.
>
> The arrest was the climax of an international hunt that combined the pace of a police thriller with the prestige of a $2 million collection of books...that vanished this summer from the library of the University College, London.

In addition to special agents, the U.S. Customs Service hires inspectors, border patrol officers, pilots, chemists, import specialists, and data processing personnel. In many of the positions which must be filled by customs, a language capability is a definite plus.

For further information, write:

United States Customs Service

Headquarters Personnel Branch
1301 Constitution Avenue, NW
Washington, D.C. 20229

100 Summer Street, Suite 1819
Boston, Massachusetts 02110

6 World Trade Center
New York, New York 10048

40 South Gay Street
Baltimore, Maryland 21202

99 SE Fifth Street
Miami, Florida 33131

423 Canal Street
New Orleans, Louisiana 70112

500 Dallas Avenue
Houston, Texas 77002

P.O. Box 2071, Main Post Office
Los Angeles, California 90053

211 Main Street, Suite 1000
San Francisco, California 94105

55 East Monroe Street
Chicago, Illinois 60603

THE BUREAU OF ALCOHOL, TOBACCO, AND FIREARMS

The federal Bureau of Alcohol, Tobacco, and Firearms (BATF) is another of the U.S. government law enforcement agencies within the Department of the Treasury. In order to carry out its responsibilities, the BATF conducts undercover operations.

Special agents of the BATF investigate violations of the federal laws relating to explosives, firearms, illicit liquor, arson, and tobacco. These investigations are designed to prevent and solve bombings, to detect illegal interstate transportation of explosives and firearms, and to control illegal possession of these items by the criminal element. Also enforced are various laws governing possession of machine guns, destructive devices, and other weapons subject to registration. Special agents work to prevent or detect illicit traffic in liquor or tobacco products and the diversion of raw materials to use in illicit production of distilled spirits (i.e., to find moonshiners and put them out of business). The BATF campaign against organized arson has grown in recent years, and investigations have increased.

The BATF spells out potential job duties to employee applicants:

> Typically, these investigations involve surveillance; participation in raids; interviewing suspects and witnesses; making arrests; obtaining search warrants and searching for physical evidence. Agents maintain close working relationships with other Federal, State and local law enforcement agencies to assist in the fight against crime and violence.
>
> When required by circumstances, the special agent must assume an undercover role and associate with known criminals to purchase contraband, observe illegal activities, and obtain additional intelligence. These investigations often involve organizations acquiring firearms and explosives through illegal means or for unlawful purposes.

As in most law enforcement activities, agents of the BATF must expect paperwork. They must review all evidence at the conclusion of an investigation, prepare a case report in many instances, and assist U.S. attorneys in the preparation and presentation of the case before and during a trial.

The duties of BATF agents frequently require irregular working hours, and involve personal risks, exposure to all kinds of weather, arduous physical exertion under rigorous conditions, as well as considerable travel. BATF personnel must expect to be stationed—and to change job locations—anywhere in the United States.

Applicants for the position of special agent must have established eligibility on the TEA examination, which includes the following basic requirements: four years of study successfully completed in a college or university or completion of all requirements for a bachelor's degree (an academic year of study is based on thirty semester hours or its equivalent); or one year of general experience and two years of specialized experience in responsible criminal investigation, for a total of three years. (Study successfully completed in a residential school above high school level may be substituted at the rate of one academic year of study for nine months of specialized experience.)

Applicants for special agent positions must attain a rating of at least seventy on the written TEA examination. Additional points may be added for study completed in police science or police administration subjects. (Eligibility after the examination will be for a one-year period, unless applicants submit up-to-date information about their qualifications within that twelve-month period.)

The Office of Personnel Management will submit to the BATF a list of the applicants who achieve high scores on the examination. Those who are referred will be interviewed and rated on the basis of appearance, manner, ability to speak, and the ability to adapt to group situations. If an applicant successfully completes the interview, he must expect to wait for several weeks while a full background investigation is conducted.

An applicant must be an American citizen; at least twenty-one, but under thirty-five years of age at the time of appointment; able to pass a complete background investigation; and in excellent physical condition. Applicants must pass a comprehensive medical examination by a licensed physician before appointment. Distant vision without correction must test at least 20/40 in each eye. Weight "must be in proportion to height." (No waiver on these requirements is granted.)

Appointees to BATF will join other new agents of various agencies for about eight weeks of intensive training in general law enforcement and investigative techniques at the consolidated Federal Law Enforcement Training Center in Glynco, Georgia. Subjects of study include rules of evidence, surveillance techniques, undercover assignments, courtroom demeanor, and the use of firearms. New special agents subsequently attend Special Agents Basic School, where they receive highly specialized training in their duties as BATF agents. Subjects studied relate to the laws enforced by BATF, case report writing, firearms and explosives nomenclature, bomb scene search, and illicit liquor investigation.

Employees at BATF generally enter on duty at the GS-05 level. The journeyman level for a special agent is GS-11, and selections for promotion above that level are made as vacancies occur. The minimum waiting period in each grade is one year; periodic within-grade step increases are provided for agents who are not promoted.

Personnel policies and benefits at BATF are generally the same as in other similar agencies; special agents are eligible for retirement at age fifty if they have twenty years' service in the criminal investigative field.

In special circumstances of unusual hardship or danger, BATF agents earn premium pay, not to exceed 25 percent of their base pay.

Those who wish to apply for BATF employment should write to one of the bureau's regional personnel offices throughout the United States. It is recommended that you apply at the regional office which serves the part of the country in which you would prefer to work:

North Atlantic Region (includes Maine, New Hampshire, Massachusetts, Connecticut, Rhode Island, New York, Vermont, New Jersey, Pennsylvania, Delaware, Maryland, Virginia, District of Columbia, and Puerto Rico):

Bureau of Alcohol, Tobacco, and Firearms
6 World Trade Center
Sixth Floor
New York, New York 10048

Southeast Region (includes Tennessee, North Carolina, South Carolina, Georgia, Alabama, Mississippi, and Florida):

Bureau of Alcohol, Tobacco, and Firearms
3835 Northeast Expressway
Atlanta, Georgia 30340

Midwest Region (includes Michigan, Indiana, Ohio, West Virginia, Kentucky, Illinois, Iowa, Nebraska, Kansas, Missouri, Minnesota, Wisconsin, North Dakota, and South Dakota):

Bureau of Alcohol, Tobacco, and Firearms
230 South Dearborn, 15th Floor
Chicago, Illinois 60604

Southwest Region (includes Wyoming, Colorado, New Mexico, Oklahoma, Texas, Arkansas, and Louisiana):

Bureau of Alcohol, Tobacco, and Firearms
Main Tower, Room 345
1200 Main Street
Dallas, Texas 75202

Western Region (includes Washington, Oregon, California, Nevada, Arizona, Utah, Idaho, Montana, Alaska, and Hawaii):

Bureau of Alcohol, Tobacco, and Firearms
525 Market Street
34th Floor
San Francisco, California 94105

A HISTORICAL NOTE

The BATF operated under a cloud of uncertainty and the morale of its agents plummeted after the election of Pres. Ronald Reagan in 1980. The bureau had long been a target of the powerful National Rifle Association and others who advocate the right to freely carry firearms, because gun registration enforcement is one of BATF's responsibilities. During his campaign, Reagan pledged to abolish BATF and, after his election, the administration announced that BATF functions would be transferred to the Secret Service and other agencies in the Department of the Treasury. But the National Rifle Association opposed *that* plan, fearing the Secret Service might enforce gun laws even more vigorously than BATF. Thus, the bureau survived.

On March 30, 1981, the head of BATF's Gun Tracing Division received an urgent call. "It's a Roehm, model RG14," the caller said. "Here's its serial number."

The Gun Tracing Division chief made three hurried telephone calls. It took him fourteen minutes to discover that the gun had recently been sold to a young man named John Warnock Hinckley, Jr.

IX
The Drug Enforcement Administration

A drug enforcement effort has been in place in the United States under one name or another since 1915. For many years it was known as the Bureau of Narcotics and Dangerous Drugs; for the past decade it has been called the Drug Enforcement Administration (DEA), an adjunct of the Department of Justice. It has always been a troubled agency or, as one Washington observer said, "plagued by corruption charges and often treated like the stepchild of federal law enforcement, shifted from place to place on the bureaucratic charts."

A major shift occurred in 1982 when the Reagan administration announced that the FBI would assume control of DEA operations. Previously the DEA had operated as a semi-independent agency within the Justice Department, reporting to the attorney general. Since the reorganization the DEA has reported to FBI director William H. Webster, and the acting director is a veteran FBI officer.

But the attempt to merge DEA operations within the FBI framework has been only partially successful. One reason is the difference in employment requirements between the DEA and the FBI. FBI agents must be college graduates, and the typical agent is a well-dressed man or woman of quiet demeanor. There is a joke in the FBI: "An FBI agent's idea of going undercover is taking off his tie." FBI officials are in a special employee category called "excepted service," and can be hired and fired by the FBI director without the protection of normal civil service considerations.

DEA agents are civil service employees, and a college degree is not required for employment. Fairly or unfairly, they are often seen as second-class enforcement citizens with an image tainted by corruption charges often headlined in the press. When an urbane FBI agent, Francis M. Mullen, Jr., was assigned in 1982 to head the DEA, his colleagues asked, according to the *Washington Post*, "Why...would a perfectly sane man in the top tier of the bureau's leadership leave to direct a group of agents who often look and act more like dope dealers than federal lawmen?"

One reason that DEA agents dress informally is that it is not practical to identify and apprehend narcotics dealers while wearing a white shirt and tie. The work of the DEA agent is difficult and risky—unquestionably the most dangerous undercover work in which any federal agent can become involved.

Since the 1982 reorganization at DEA, morale in the agency has declined. Agents have wondered if they would be fired and replaced with FBI agents or taken over by the larger bureau, which has four times as many operatives than the 1,800 agents at DEA. The agency has also been unsettled by the fact that FBI agent Francis Mullen, Jr. had to wait eighteen months for Senate confirmation in his post as DEA chief. Such a delay would not occur at other federal bureaus.

One symptom of the disorganization that plagues DEA becomes obvious to young people who enquire about employment in the agency. It is difficult to obtain information about qualifications required and the responsibilities expected of those who wish to become DEA agents. One applicant wrote two letters asking for recruitment literature and did not receive a reply to either; nor did he hear again after a high-level DEA official promised during a telephone conversation to mail to him an employment application. (A good first step is to fill out a government Standard Form 171 and deliver it personally to the nearest DEA office, the location of which can be found under the Department of Justice listing in the telephone book.)

In addition to its responsibility for investigating illegal narcotics activities in the United States, the DEA attempts to thwart the efforts of criminals who smuggle dangerous drugs into this country from abroad. Thus, many DEA agents are assigned to overseas posts. The work is dangerous. For example, it was reported on February 11, 1983, in the *Washington Post* that "two agents of the federal Drug Enforcement Agency were shot Tuesday night near Cartagena, Colombia, after five men posing as Colombian policemen broke into their hotel room and dragged them into the jungle at gunpoint...." (DEA is often referred to, inaccurately, as the Drug Enforcement Agency.)

In short, the DEA is an agency involved in the criminal investigation of narcotics dealers and the enforcement of narcotics laws. It is a rough and tough occupation which will probably not be rewarding for the average young person interested in undercover work. Applicants without a college degree and with police experience, however, might be more at home in the DEA.

X
The Department of State

The Bureau of Intelligence and Research (INR) is a small, specialized intelligence unit within the Department of State. It has no agents—except in the sense that all Department of State officers abroad report political intelligence—and it conducts no clandestine operations. INR's officers are all Department of State personnel, most of them foreign service officers on home tours. The director is usually an ambassador serving in INR as a part of his career in the Department of State.

INR produces political and some economic intelligence reports to meet the Department of State's needs. It also coordinates the department's relations with U.S. foreign intelligence organizations and disseminates reports received from U.S. diplomatic and consular posts abroad. An INR officer is always a senior participant in the production of National Intelligence Estimates (NIEs), which are interagency predictions of political stability and military intentions of foreign countries.

Employment in INR is generally available only to those who have already become Department of State officers, the senior analysts usually being persons who have served abroad. Entrance requirements for foreign service officer careers in the Department of State are stringent: good academic credentials and the ability to pass tough, competitive written and oral exams.

Some sobering statistics: of the 16,829 candidates who took the most recent four-hour written test, only 2,587 passed. Of that number, more than 2,000 are expected to fail the day-long oral assessment exams that follow. Of the approximately 500 who survive the orals, about 125 will be eliminated by medical or security checks, or be lured to higher-paying jobs in private industry during the several months of waiting for admission to training courses at the Foreign Service Institute.

More than half of the institute's most recent graduates had master's degrees; 1 in 10 was a lawyer; 1 in 20 held a doctorate; and about half had skills in a foreign language.

Unlike many departments, the age limit for entering the foreign service is sixty years old; thus many applicants have previous work experience.

XI
If You Don't Have a College Degree

It is usually simple to provide guidance to young people who aspire to careers in intelligence if they have special qualifications, appropriate experience or area knowledge, or a foreign language talent—and a college degree.

But often, a would-be intelligence officer does not have a college degree. One young man wrote: "I've tried CIA, the FBI and half-a-dozen other agencies. No luck at all. It appears you must cover yourself first with a sheepskin if you want to wear a cloak and carry a dagger." As an indication of his frustration, the young man enclosed a paragraph from a 1983 *New York Times* article about the CIA with particular passages emphasized: "*A quarter of a million Americans*, many of whom saw the CIA's sophisticated ('We May Have a Career for You!') recruiting ads in newspapers and magazines, got in touch with the agency about jobs last year. *Ten thousand*, most in their late 20's with *college degrees* and experience in fields that involve foreign affairs, submitted formal applications and *1,500 were hired*."

With such intense competition among college graduates, it is clear that becoming an intelligence officer without a college degree is not easy. But it can be done. Many intelligence officers advance to officer rank because of demonstrated ability while serving as less-senior employees, much the same way that enlisted personnel in the military services become officers after on-the-job or after-hours education, or are appointed to officer rank with "battlefield promotions."

The vast majority of job openings in the various agencies and departments that conduct secret operations are for employees, not officers, in positions that do not require college or university training.

For instance, in Chapter VII an advertisement seeking applicants for army intelligence was quoted: "Jobs. Army Intelligence in Arlington,

Virginia, has openings for engineers, illustrators and intelligence specialists, Grades GS-07 through GS-12." The first position is the kind that calls for an officer candidate, civilian or military, with a college degree; obviously the Defense Intelligence Agency will not hire self-trained engineers. The second category, illustrators, represents one of the literally hundreds of jobs available to persons with specialized skills regardless of educational background. The third category, intelligence specialists, is one which includes scores of intelligence positions that require nothing beyond a high school education and, in a few instances, not even that: proficiency in weapons maintenance and bomb disposal, for example.

One good question for young people without a college degree is, "How's your typing?"

In the CIA, male and female typists, stenographers, and couriers must be 17½ years of age, U.S. citizens, and high school graduates. Secretaries may be assigned overseas at age twenty-one. Some of the foreign assignments are certainly challenging, especially when a tour in Latin America in a hardship post is followed by a subsequent assignment to the jungles of Southeast Asia. There are other jobs to be filled, of course, in Rome, Paris, and other world capitals.

CIA's recruitment literature for those seeking clerical positions makes the following promises:

> In the course of your career you will have opportunities for varied work experiences and advancement. The Office of Training offers courses which can assist in preparing you to assume positions of greater responsibility. For example, certain areas of study include administrative procedures, effective writing, employee development, or supervision and management. If you are to serve overseas, you may participate in language training. Evening and part-time courses in a variety of subjects are offered in an after-hours, off-campus program at the Headquarters Building. Tuition costs for approved job-related training will be borne by the Agency. By enhancing your qualifications through experience and training, you can realistically aspire to advance to higher administrative positions.

The promises are not empty. Many of the female reports officers and operations officers in the CIA graduated from secretarial ranks. A number of intelligence officers obtained their degrees, sometimes advanced degrees, while staying on the job during the day and attending school at night.

Therefore, for those without a college degree but who are determined to work in intelligence careers, a developed skill and on-the-job training will help them become employees of the CIA, FBI, NSA, or one of the other services. Once hired, the opportunity exists in these agencies and departments to advance. In intelligence jargon this is known as developing "upward career mobility." It requires hard work and some luck. (But remember baseball manager Branch Rickey's definition: "Luck is the residue of design.")

In my own case, I served overseas for the CIA in eight countries, on four assignments as chief of station. When I retired from the CIA, I was managing a budget of many millions of dollars and CIA operations in some twenty countries. I was a GS-18, highest career ranking in the federal bureaucracy except for certain executive appointments.

Since retiring from the CIA, I've often thought about going to college as more and more mature people do these days to obtain the college degree I've never had.

XII
Equal Employment Opportunity
in U.S. Intelligence

A United States senator once expressed surprise during a CIA briefing when he learned of a woman officer. "Do you have women working at CIA?" he asked.

Today one out of three CIA employees is female; 32 percent to be exact. Many are secretaries, but clerical duties overseas can be stimulating, and there are times when a secretary leaves her desk in an official installation and participates in such clandestine activities as stakeouts or surveillance. Women also serve in the United States and abroad as analysts, reports officers, and, increasingly, as case officers.

After I joined the CIA in 1950, my first overseas supervisor—my case officer—was a woman. Later, during my first headquarters tour in 1954, my chief was a woman who had an artificial leg. In the OSS in World War II, she had to remove the leg and strap it to her body when she parachuted behind enemy lines in France.

The number of female case officers working for the CIA abroad has increased significantly in recent years. In some situations women perform better as managers of spies than men. In the Middle East, for instance, an Arab agent can rationalize his treason to his own country when working for a woman case officer because in his mind a mere female cannot be taken seriously. In Latin America, a female case officer can approach and cultivate a potential spy easily, because few Latins really believe the CIA would employ a woman for tasks of such delicacy and importance.

Because of the need for language fluency and for agents who can blend into international backgrounds, there has always been a sizable contingent of ethnic groups in the CIA, especially Orientals and persons of Hispanic heritage. Some years ago four CIA officers died in two separate helicopter crashes in Southeast Asia—one was a black, another was a full-blooded American Indian.

Blacks today often prefer to find careers in agencies where their employment is overt and their successes can be publicly acknowledged rather than at the CIA or NSA, where their work is so sensitive it cannot be discussed with family and friends. It is understandable that blacks, after more than two centuries of opportunity denied to them, seek employment which allows their talent and advancement to be recognized. That is not possible in an undercover role. Nevertheless, a number of dedicated blacks have worked as intelligence officers abroad.

Affirmative action programs are now mandatory at all U.S. intelligence agencies, and each agency must make an annual report of its progress to the Equal Employment Opportunity Commission. Consequently the number of minority employees in the intelligence community has increased dramatically, and the opportunities for minorities seeking entry level jobs are greater than ever.

The FBI is a prime example. Under J. Edgar Hoover, chief of the bureau for forty-two years, the FBI was an organization of white men run by white men. When William Webster became the director in 1978, there were very few blacks, Orientals, Indians, or Hispanics among the FBI's special agents. Of the 1,200 new agents recruited in Webster's first three years, 94 were blacks, 19 Hispanics, 19 Orientals, and 8 were Indians. A cadre of 91 female agents was increased to 350. In one year the San Francisco field office of the FBI hired 16 new agents, only two of which were white males.

"We had really not been recruiting," Director Webster told a journalist, "we'd been screeners of white male applicants. The bureau didn't know much about getting blacks and Hispanics to apply for jobs, because they didn't know how to get the word out to those groups."

The U.S. Secret Service has lagged behind other agencies in the hiring of minorities, but in recent years a number of blacks and a few women have become Secret Service agents.

The DEA is another agency where affirmative action programs have been sluggish. But in 1982, a U.S. district judge ordered DEA to pay about two million dollars in back salary to more than two hundred black agents who had been discriminated against within DEA in the previous decade. Further, the judge ordered DEA to promote one black agent for every two white agents promoted to senior levels until the percentage of black supervisors reached 10 percent.

Homosexuals continue to be considered security risks in most intelligence agencies, and are not hired if homosexual tendencies are spotted during security reviews. But even in this area there have been some changes in recent years when homosexuals obtain employment in undercover work despite pre-entry investigation. The first decision of its kind within the American intelligence community occurred in 1980 when officials of the supersecret National Security Agency allowed a middle-level employee, who admitted he was homosexual, to keep his job. He was kept on the payroll after he pledged to tell his family of his homosexuality, not to engage in public illegal acts, and maintain normal NSA anonymity.

A more recent development was in 1982 when an electronics technician, who was dismissed from the CIA after voluntarily disclosing that he was a homosexual, went to court filing a lawsuit seeking reinstatement and back pay. The man was identified in the press only as "John Doe" because of his prior undercover work. He contended that he would not be subjected to blackmail because he had acknowledged to the CIA and to his family and friends that he was gay. A court ruling—which could significantly affect present policies of intelligence agencies concerning employment of gays—has not yet been delivered.

Handicapped persons have the opportunity to work in secret operations, despite the obvious problems in some areas, such as assignment to international hot spots where mobility is essential. As CIA recruitment literature states, "In accordance with affirmative action requirements of several statutes concerning employment of individuals with handicaps, the existence of a handicap is not automatically disqualifying." The CIA, in fact, has an excellent record in employment of the handicapped, and its recruitment statement, while stiff and formal, is certainly better than the statement found in employment brochures of the U.S. Customs Service: "Persons with a hearing aid, noticeable deformities or disfiguring conditions should not apply."

Despite slow progress in a few areas, women, minorities, and the handicapped can presently expect fair treatment in U.S. intelligence agencies and the opportunity for advancement to senior positions. Today one of the eleven associate directors of the FBI is a black special agent, and it is no longer a rarity to find women and minorities in the senior ranks of the military intelligence establishment. Also, it is no longer a surprise when a woman is appointed as an overseas chief of station for the CIA, as it was a decade ago, when I nominated the first female for that position.

XIII
Ethics and Morality—
And Secret Operations

In Chapter IV there was an examination of dirty tricks in the context of covert action, a discussion of the institutional issue of government morality.

There is also a personal dimension involved in the dilemma of secret operations in a free and open society such as ours. The question of personal ethics seldom arises in the case of intelligence officers who are overt, who identify themselves and, often, the kind of work they do when talking with friends and neighbors. The majority of intelligence operatives fall into this category.

But the undercover officer—usually those in the Directorate of Operations in the CIA—sometimes finds that the job demands standards of conduct that fall into a gray area and pose problems of personal ethics for the individual.

This was brought home to me when I found myself in a situation where my cover could have been revealed by a U.S. president. John F. Kennedy visited Mexico City in 1962, a year before his assassination in Dallas. I was posted to the U.S. embassy in Mexico City at the time, under diplomatic cover. In that cover capacity, I attended a reception for President Kennedy; some two thousand people were on hand when he arrived.

When Kennedy entered the ballroom, he was followed by a pack of about forty reporters and photographers. Like any good politician, he began to shake hands. Suddenly the president headed straight for me. He put out his hand.

"Hi!" said the president of the United States. "I'm Jack Kennedy."

"Sir." We shook hands. "I'm David Phillips."

"What do you do here, Mr. Phillips, in Mexico?"

Behind Kennedy the reporters were making notes, and flashbulbs were popping.

"I work for you, Mr. President. In the embassy."

"I see." Obviously Kennedy wanted a better answer. "What do you do in the embassy, Mr. Phillips?"

I continued to equivocate; the President became clearly impatient—he insisted on knowing precisely what I did at the embassy.

How could I reply truthfully? And yet, could I lie to my own commander in chief? Even with the excuse that flashbulbs were blinking and reporters were writing down everything I said?

Fortunately, in this instance the military attaché assigned to the embassy came to my rescue. He knew what I really did, tugged at Kennedy's coattails, and whispered in his ear. The president then said in a loud voice, "Very well, Mr. Phillips. Carry on." He then continued his round shaking hands with others who had no problems in answering his questions.

The dilemmas found in the conduct of clandestine activities in our free and open society are not always so easily resolved. Secrecy. Double lives. Illegal acts.

Some people honestly believe that there should be no secrecy in our government operations. But those who must conduct our affairs, national and international, always believe, or eventually conclude, that secrecy is essential. George Washington wrote in a letter to his aide, Col. Elias Dayton, "The necessity for procuring good intelligence is apparent and need not be further urged—all that remains for me to add is that you keep the whole matter as secret as possible. For upon secrecy, success depends in most enterprises of the kind and for want of it, they are generally defeated, however well planned." Henry L. Stimson was the U.S. secretary of state in 1929 when he abolished the famous "Black Chamber," the nation's codebreaking organization, with the declaration, "Gentlemen don't read other peoples' mail." Ten years later, however, Stimson became the secretary of war (today, the secretary of defense) and promptly called for the re-establishment of codebreaking operations. He had learned, as all our leaders do sooner or later, that nongentlemen run affairs in many parts of the world. At home, secrecy has long been recognized as essential, even in peacetime. The law provides criminal penalties for the unauthorized disclosure of such government information as future crop estimates from the Department of Agriculture, identities of recipients of federal welfare, income tax information, selective service records, applicants for Land Bank loans, and formulas for insecticides. And in 1981, intelligence professionals were pleased when a new law finally was added to the list, making it a crime to reveal the identities of intelligence officers under cover.

While a majority of intelligence people have not been inhibited about concerns of secrecy, some of those who have worked in clandestine activities have been uncomfortable in the face of the demands of living a double life. This is seldom a concern abroad where it is absolutely essential to maintain and protect cover. In most parts of the world the undercover officer cannot perform effectively unless his identity and true functions are concealed; in some areas he is in peril if his cover is not hermetically maintained.

Intelligence officers who must depend on their covers to conduct business abroad are obliged to continue the covers at home so that it will be intact when they are again assigned overseas. This kind of double life, in one's own community, is difficult. Undercover operatives must pretend to be somewhere else when a creditor or visitor from out of town telephones them at the office at CIA headquarters on an outside line (that is, not tied into the CIA switchboard). If troubled, they may not select their own psychiatrist, but instead must visit one cleared and approved by the CIA. They, and their families, must lie constantly. They cannot tell the truth to bankers, neighbors, lodge brothers, or delivery boys. I even lied to the Boy Scouts of America when filling out the application papers to be a scoutmaster. It is a vexing existence, but one to which most men and women can adjust successfully.

Even more difficult is the fact that in undercover intelligence work it is sometimes necessary to commit illegal acts, or acts that can be perceived as illegal by others. An example: a case officer preparing to depart for an overseas assignment where he or she will pretend to be a businessperson must first obtain an unofficial U.S. passport. In doing so, it is necessary to violate U.S. law in the sense that the passport application must be completed with less-than-truthful answers to some questions. Once abroad the intelligence operative must perform various tasks which violate local legal rules. There are circumstances in which the intelligence officer must resort to tactics (bribery, for instance) which he would never consider attempting at home. Such personal-level dirty tricks aspects of foreign intelligence work are in contradiction to American principles of fair play. Unless the operative can accommodate the double standards, which espionage activity sometimes requires, the job simply will not get done.

While he was not addressing undercover activity specifically, Abraham Lincoln understood this gray area of government service when he said in a speech to the Thirtieth Congress in 1848:

> The true rule in determining to embrace or reject anything is not whether it have *any* evil in it, but whether it have more evil than good. Almost everything, especially of government policy, is an inseperable compound of the two; so that our best judgement of the

preponderance between them is continually demanded. On this principle, the President, his friends, and the world generally, act on most subjects. Why not apply it then, upon this question?... Why, as to this magnify the *evil*, and stoutly refuse to see any good in them?

Professional intelligence officers—after pondering the problems of secret operations in our democratic society and their personal role in it—invariably reach the conclusion that performance in espionage is not only essential but honorable. John Le Carré writes of *The Honourable Schoolboy*; William E. Colby's memoirs carry the title *Honorable Men*. The first American spy, Nathan Hale, said before he was executed by the British: "I wish to be useful. And every kind of service, necessary to the public good, becomes honorable by being necessary."

Any person contemplating a career in the clandestine arena should enter the profession fully aware that covert action and espionage carry personal challenges with them. The great majority of those who enter the profession find that their sense of morality and personal ethics remains intact. And most undercover operatives find their careers to be rewarding.

In 1983, the *Washington Post* conducted a survey of more than 58,000 government workers. Each employee was asked to indicate in written, anonymous responses how he or she felt about job satisfaction. Some agencies and departments were given poor grades, and employees were unhappy enough to say they would not sign up again with Uncle Sam if given the opportunity. Among the organizations in which morale was low were the Labor Department, Office of Personnel Management, General Services Administration, Environmental Protection Agency, and the Interior Department. Four organizations ranked above the dozens of agencies in the federal bureaucracy in the opinion of the people who worked in them: the navy, the Veteran's Administration, the Export-Import Bank—and the CIA.

XIV
Federal Retirement

Government employees have a percentage of each paycheck deducted toward eventual retirement. The amount of an annuity is based on a formula calling for a specified number of years of creditable service—those years of federal service in the military plus civilian employment during years in which deductions toward retirement were made. In some cases—the CIA, FBI, and foreign service of the Department of State—funds withheld go into a non-civil service account. Should an employee in one of these systems resign or be dismissed before accumulating enough years to retire, he or she will receive a lump sum payment which can be transferred to the civil service annuity system, and the years worked will be credited toward a civil service pension at age sixty-two (at a reduced rate) or sixty-five (for a full annuity).

Military pensions are quite generous, and deductions toward retirement are not taken from paychecks. According to a 1983 study the average pension benefit for military retirees—87 percent of whom are under the age of sixty-five—is almost three times higher than most private sector plans. Some military personnel are eligible for retirement in their late thirties or early forties. Thus many retired military people, enlisted persons as well as officers, enjoy financial stability while seeking second careers.

A SPECIAL RETIREMENT SITUATION

There is a long-range, potential problem which should be considered by persons who are hired to work for U.S. intelligence on an informal basis, or with a contract that does not stipulate that time served is creditable, and for which annuity deductions are not made. This problem arises in cases where operatives are under cover or in deep cover. If they later find themselves working in an overt capacity for the government, they may not benefit from the years of undercover employment. In some cases their tasks have been so secret that they are not allowed to notify the Office of Personnel Management to have the time served credited toward civil service annuities. An example: For some years the Office of Naval Intelligence managed a very secret task force in which the officers were independent contractors, and no deductions toward retirement were taken from their salaries. Then the supersecret unit was disbanded. Twenty-two of the deep-cover operatives later found jobs elsewhere in the government as civilians. After some years, they sought retirement credit for their undercover years, asking the Office of Personnel Management to rule that the secret work they did for the navy qualified as creditable years toward retirement as federal workers. Their claim was rejected because they had been independent contractors, and because no records could be produced that proved the operatives had really been employed in the secret task force!

The chief administrative law judge of the Merit Systems Protection Board acknowledged that "Civil Service documentation would have been unwise, even dangerous." But he ruled that the years worked for the navy were nevertheless creditable.

But that decision was overturned in a higher court. To date the twenty-two intelligence operatives have not been able to benefit from their undercover years.

In many cases intelligence services will not grant creditable years to contract operatives, such benefits being reserved for staff personnel. But the independent contractor in undercover positions should attempt to have the obligation written into his contract if the prospect of future federal employment in an overt role is anticipated.

POSTRETIREMENT CAREERS AND CAMARADERIE

In the past former intelligence operatives, like old soldiers, "simply faded away" into quiet second careers or retirement obscurity in a life which precluded public recognition of their years of silent service.

Times have changed. After the information explosion about secret operations and a new openness about the role of intelligence in our society, former agents now frequently have visible second careers, and they gather together in professional or social organizations to continue the companionship they enjoyed in intelligence agencies.

Intelligence people with a background of language knowledge and foreign expertise garnered during overseas assignments sometimes find satisfactory second careers as teachers. Former FBI special agents often become local political figures, lawyers, and judges. Operatives with technical backgrounds are recruited for the expanding U.S. high tech industries. A surprisingly large number of former intelligence men and women perform volunteer community tasks.

Whether they work or concentrate on leisure activities, former intelligence personnel enthusiastically participate in a number of alumni organizations. Among them are:

1. Association of Former Intelligence Officers (AFIO), a national organization of former operatives from all services dedicated to defending and promoting a strong United States intelligence service as vital to national security. AFIO conducts research, provides speakers to grassroots organizations, offers professional testimony to congressional committees on intelligence legislation, and publishes a newsletter and a series of monographs on intelligence.

2. Society of Former Special Agents of the FBI is a national group of some 8,000 former bureau operatives. This is a politically potent organization active in Washington and throughout the country.

3. Central Intelligence Retirees Association (CIRA) is primarily a social and fraternal group of former CIA personnel who gather to remember old times and compete with each other on the golf course.

4. National Military Intelligence Association (NMIA) seeks to enhance the craft of intelligence in the military services. Membership is composed of active as well as retired officers and enlisted personnel.

5. National Intelligence Study Center (NISC) is a Washington-based organization which attempts to improve academic and journalistic understanding of the role of intelligence.

The above is only a partial listing of the organizations of former intelligence officers who renew their professional relationships after retirement. Some of the groups are small, dedicated to a single purpose. One example is an organization that raises funds for the Richard S. Welch Memorial Fund at Harvard to finance studies in intelligence at the John F. Kennedy School of Government and the Center for International Affairs. (Richard Welch was assassinated in Athens after his identity was revealed by CIA critic Philip Agee.)

A review of the upcoming chapter on intelligence literature demonstrates that a sizable number of former operatives have become writers. The burgeoning number has resulted in a new social phenomenon—former spook literati. The National Intelligence Study Center even hands out annual prizes for merit in intelligence literature.

Former intelligence officers no longer fade away, but enjoy the camaraderie of long-standing friendships socially and contribute professionally to U.S. society.

XV
The Intelligence Agent's Language

Spies and counterspies have developed their own jargon, and uninitiated eavesdroppers would be baffled when listening to the dialogue between intelligence operatives. Many of the words and terms used in secret operations have been explained in the text of this book (e.g., *case officer*). The following narrative is about an imaginary CIA case officer, Jim Sears.

In his overseas operations, Jim Sears prepares to conduct his business by *putting in the plumbing*. The *plumbing* is the support structure that must be installed so that Jim's intelligence activity can be carried out, usually by the establishment of a cover facility, emergency contact arrangements with agents, and secure ways to communicate with them.

In addition to his own *cover*—the installation or activity that explains Jim's presence in a country abroad—he will need a *safe house* where he can meet his agents. This will be an office or apartment procured in such a manner that it cannot be linked to Jim or to the agents he meets there clandestinely. He will also obtain one or more *drops* (e.g., a hole in an old tree, the tank of a public commode, a hollowed out brick) where he can deposit and retrieve communications from agents without actually meeting them. If Jim Sears's agents travel abroad, they may communicate with him by way of an *accommodation address*, a mail address, usually a post office box. Messages cached in a drop or sent to an accommodation address are usually in *secret writing (SW)*, that is, written with an invisible substance, ranging from lemon juice to sophisticated chemicals that appear under certain conditions. If the agent is in another country where strict security conditions prevail, he may send his messages to Jim by radio. For maximum safety the agent will use a *burst transmission*—a preset message transmitted so quickly on an agent radio that it thwarts hostile direction finding surveillance.

As a case officer, Jim Sears is a manager of spies. Some of his agents are volunteers, *walk-ins*, usually foreigners who enter an embassy to offer their services. Others Jim must recruit with a *pitch*, the act of persuading a person to be an agent. If the subject is approached without prior cultivation, it is known as a *cold pitch*. A *false flag* recruitment involves a deliberate misrepresentation of one's actual employer to achieve the recruitment. An English-speaking KGB officer who pretends to be British, for instance, and approaches an agent-candidate would be attempting a false flag recruitment.

Jim Sears will be alert for someone who can serve as a *principal agent*, one who recruits and manages a network of subagents. He will also be on the lookout for one or more *agents of influence*, local personalities who can influence political developments or can manipulate an opinion maker. Jim will also attempt to recruit other agents for specialized tasks. One, for instance, might be a *dangle*, someone intentionally brought to the attention of a hostile intelligence service, as a device to learn more about the enemy. He may need an agent capable of installing a *bug*, a surreptitiously placed radio transmitter, in the headquarters of a local terrorist group. That would require a *listening post*, a secure area from which transmissions from the bug can be monitored.

In all his dealings with his agents, Jim Sears will adhere to strict *tradecraft*, the professional conduct that will prevent a *flap*, the publicity or controversy that ensues in the wake of a botched intelligence operation. He will be alert for a *danger signal*, an indicator that a clandestine meeting should be aborted, such as a chalk mark on a wall. Jim will be sure his agents carry the proper *pocket litter*, the misleading documents and materials an agent has to protect his identity and background should he be apprehended. He will frequently *flutter* or *box* his agents—conduct lie detector examinations. This is one of several precautions Jim will take to be sure his man or woman has not become a *double agent* who is pretending loyalty to Jim while actually in the pay of another. (As a verb, *double* means to "turn" a hostile agent so that he will report on his employers.) Jim Sears will also be alert to the possibility his agent has become a *fabricator* who provides false information. If this is done consistently and in volume, the agent's duplicity is known as a *paper mill*.

Jim Sears or one of his colleagues may sometimes be involved in *black* propaganda, an activity that claims to originate, falsely, with a real or imagined source. An example would be a clandestine radio broadcast supposedly made by jungle-based rebels. If no attribution is provided, such propaganda is described as *gray*.

Less interesting, but absolutely essential to intelligence work, is *surveillance*. Jim will spend much of his time overseas supervising the systematic observation or monitoring of places, persons, or things by visual, aural, electronic, photographic, or other means.

All of Jim Sears's activities are undertaken so that he can produce intelligence. HUMINT, information from a person (i.e., human intelligence), is a major category in the product Jim sends back to CIA headquarters at Langley, Virginia. Another variety—among many—is COMINT, the intelligence gathered from communications or the activities that protect communications. SIGINT (signals) and ELINT (electronic) are associated with COMINT. Will outer space espionage become known as SPAINT?

Good tradecraft demands that Jim dedicate himself to good *counter-intelligence*—an intelligence service's activities to protect itself from attempts to weaken it or from hostile *penetrations*. Penetration is the method used to discover the secrets of an adversary intelligence agency: a listening device, deciphering of codes, or the burrowing of a *mole*, a high-level penetrator who can provide the innermost secrets of one intelligence service to a hostile service. The term was not used by modern operatives until John Le Carré popularized it in his espionage novels. (CIA historian Walter Pforzheimer discovered the following in Sir Francis Bacon's 1622 history of King Henry VII: "Hee was carefull and liberall to obtaine good Intelligence from all parts abroad. . . . He had such Moles perpetually working and casting to undermine him.")

Jim Sears has a top-priority task to fulfill while conducting his secret business abroad: to learn as much as he can about the intelligence operations of the Soviet Union. He monitors the activities of the KGB, the Russian Committee of State Security, the agency responsible for foreign and domestic intelligence. He keeps an eye on the GRU, Chief Intelligence Directorate of the Soviet General Staff, the military espionage organization. He carefully observes the activity of the *resident*, the chief Soviet intelligence officer in a country outside the Soviet Union, the counterpart of Jim's own CIA chief of station. And he attempts to uncover the operations of Soviet *illegals* who do not use official cover. When such an operative waits for many years to begin his activity, he is known as a *sleeper*.

Jim Sears uses the above words and terms (and dozens more) during his day on the intelligence beat.

XVI
What to Read

To absorb the literature of secret operations it would be necessary to begin with the 500 B.C. writing of Sun Tzu, the Bible, the histories of European services, and the many books about intelligence operations during the American Revolution and Civil War.

A more practical approach is to begin with World War II. I recommend the following, to be read in the order listed if feasible. First, *The Quiet Canadian: The Secret Service Story of Sir William Stephenson*, by British writer H. Montgomery Hyde. Quite reliable, it is also very readable. It is the story of a British masterspy, Sir William Stephenson, code name Intrepid. (London: Hamish Hamilton, 1962; published in the United States under the title *Room 3603: The Story of the British Intelligence Center in New York during World War II*, New York: Farrar, Straus & Co., 1963.) For the wartime exploits of American agents, read Joseph Persico's *Piercing the Reich: The Penetration of Nazi Germany by American Secret Agents During World War II*. Persico describes the strategic and tactical operations of the OSS in Germany and Austria. (New York: Viking Press, 1979; paperback, Ballantine Books, 1979.) Then there is *The Double-Cross System in the War of 1939 to 1945*, by Sir John Masterman. It describes the highly complex and successful efforts by British intelligence to neutralize, and in many cases to utilize, the services of every German agent in Britain during World War II. (New Haven: Yale University Press, 1972; paperback, New York: Ballantine Espionage/Intelligence Library, 1982.) And, finally, *Ultra Goes to War*, by Ronald Lewin, is the story of prewar Polish and French intelligence service contributions to the eventual breaking of Enigma by the British, and how the possession of the Ultra material—the deciphered messages of the German military command—made a major contribution to the Allied victory. (New York: McGraw-Hill, 1978; paperback, Pocket Books, 1981.)

There are dozens of books about the CIA. Of special interest to historians and students is *Donovan and the CIA: A History of the Establishment* of the Central Intelligence Agency, by Thomas F. Troy. This is the definitive account of OSS chief "Wild Bill" Donovan and his contributions to the founding of the CIA. (Frederick, Maryland: Aletheia Books, University Publications of America, 1981.) The Craft of Intelligence is by Allen Welsh Dulles, America's most famous CIA officer. Dulles, a former director of the CIA, writes of U.S. espionage operations during the time he headed the agency, until he was forced to resign because of the Bay of Pigs fiasco. (New York: Harper and Row, 1963; paperback, Signet Books, New American Library, 1965.) The Real CIA, by Lyman B. Kirkpatrick, Jr., is an early book on CIA operations and the agency's role in U.S. government by a man who was a senior intelligence officer until he retired to become a political science professor. (New York: Macmillan, 1968.) Ray S. Cline is the author of The CIA: Under Reagan, Bush & Casey, an update of Cline's 1976 Secrets, Spies and Scholars, written with authority by a man who was once chief of the Department of State's INR and a deputy director of the CIA. (Washington, D.C.: Acropolis Books, 1981.)

Honorable Men: My Life in the CIA, by William E. Colby, is the memoir of the director of Central Intelligence who was at the helm during the stormy weather of intelligence community investigations. Colby also writes of his role as an ambassador in Vietnam and the pacification and Phoenix programs there. (New York: Simon and Schuster, 1978.) Facing Reality: From World Federalism to the CIA, by Cord Meyer, is an important and carefully written book; Meyer was the chief of the CIA's covert action operations against the Soviet Union. (New York: Harper & Row, 1980.) More background on Soviet operations can be found in Harry Rositzke's CIA's Secret Operations (New York: Reader's Digest Press, 1977) and William Hood's Mole. Hood recounts the story of CIA spy Maj. Pytor Popov whose reports, Hood estimates, saved the United States "half a billion dollars in military research." (New York: Norton, 1982; paperback, Ballantine Books, 1983.) The human role in intelligence operations, especially in CIA's Directorate of Operations, can be found in my own The Night Watch. (New York: Atheneum, 1977; paperback, Ballantine Espionage/Intelligence Library, 1982.)

The CIA books recommended above were all written by loyalists who, while sometimes raising questions, generally advocate a strong U.S. intelligence capability.

For a more objective viewpoint, read The Man Who Kept the Secrets: Richard Helms & the CIA, by Thomas Powers. This is the most comprehensive volume yet published by an outsider about the CIA, its operations, and the investigations of the agency in 1975. The subtitle is misleading: it is not the story of Richard Helms; his lengthy intelligence career is used as a skeleton on which Powers fleshes out the CIA story.

It is well written and well researched. (New York: Alfred A. Knopf, 1979; paperback, Pocket Books, 1981.)

For a subjective, quite negative view of the CIA, read two books by former agents who have been critics. *Inside the Company: A CIA Diary*, by Philip Agee, is an exposé and bitter denunciation of the agency by the man who has made a career of revealing the identities of intelligence operatives. (New York: Stonehill, 1975; paperback, Bantam Books, 1976.) Also read *The CIA and the Cult of Intelligence*, another opposing view by Victor Marchetti and John Marks. Marchetti is a former CIA officer; Marks once worked in INR. (New York: Alfred A. Knopf, 1974; paperback, Dell, 1983.)

Two books provide information on the FBI. *The FBI Story*, by Don Whitehead, is a dated but readable account of early FBI achievements. (New York: Random House, 1956.) A solid, modern study can be found in the more recent *FBI: An Uncensored Look Behind the Walls*, by Sanford J. Ungar. (Boston: Atlantic, Little, Brown, 1976.)

Codes, codebreakers, and the NSA are the subjects of three important books on America's most secret intelligence operations. For a historical perspective, read *The American Black Chamber*, by Herbert Osborn Yardley. Yardley reveals early U.S. codebreaking efforts before they were closed down by Secretary of State Stimson. A classic work and long out of print (Indianapolis: Bobbs-Merrill, 1931), it is now available in paperback. (New York: Ballantine Espionage/Intelligence Library, 1981.) *The Codebreakers*, by David Kahn, is the best book ever written on the subject. Kahn is the recognized authority on ciphers. His book describes the evolution of the organizations involved in cryptology; sixty pages are devoted to the NSA. (New York: Macmillan, 1967; paperback, Signet Books, New American Library, 1973.) The most recent history of the NSA is *The Puzzle Palace: A Report on America's Most Secret Agency*, by James Bamford. This controversial book—because of the myriad of new secrets it reveals— was written after the author obtained numerous documents through the Freedom of Information Act. (Boston: Houghton Mifflin, 1982; paperback, New York: Penguin, 1983.)

The espionage and covert action operations of the Soviet Union have been the subjects of numerous books. A sampling which provides a good overview can be found in four books. First, *The Penkovskiy Papers*, by Oleg Penkovskiy, consists of musings by the most valuable spy to operate for the West from within a Soviet secret service. Some critics have claimed these diaries are a fabrication; in fact, they are authentic. (Garden City, New York: Doubleday, 1965; paperback, New York: Ballantine, 1982.) *My Silent War* is the memoir of Kim Philby, the most famous mole in history. Philby rose to the rank of chief of Soviet operations for the British before he was uncovered; the KGB, eternally grateful, arranged for Philby to drive one of the three Rolls-Royce automobiles in Moscow after his flight to Russia. (New York: Grove, 1968; paperback, Ballantine Espionage/ Intelligence Library, 1983.) A rare insider's view of deception and disinformation operations can be found in *The Deception Game: Czechoslovak Intelligence in Soviet Political Warfare*, by Ladislav Bittman. Bittman was a Czech intelligence officer who managed many of the operations he describes. (Syracuse, New York: Syracuse Research Corp., 1972; paperback, New York: Ballantine Espionage/Intelligence Library, 1981.) Finally, two books written by John Barron, the recognized authority on the KGB: *KGB: The Secret Work of Soviet Secret Agents*—the best book written on Russia's premier intelligence service, with detailed episodes of KGB successes and failures (New York: Reader's Digest Press, 1974; paperback, Bantam Books, 1974); and now Barron has published an updated version entitled *KGB Today: The Hidden Hand*. (New York: Reader's Digest Press, 1983.)

If you doubt what I have to say about any of these books, there is a new volume with which you should become familiar. It is a book about the books on intelligence—George C. Constantinides's *Intelligence and Espionage: An Analytical Bibliography*. (Boulder, Colorado: Westview Press, 1983.) Here Constantinides reviews, evaluates, compares, and contrasts over 500 books on the subject.

For those who really want to dig deeply into the field of intelligence literature—perhaps to answer questions, write a thesis, or write a book of your own—there is another bibliography worth consulting. It is the *Scholar's Guide to Intelligence Literature*, edited by Mrs. Marjorie Cline et al. and published by University Publications of America, Inc., Frederick, Maryland. It lists some 6,000 volumes in the Russell J. Bowen Collection at Georgetown University in Washington, D.C. Unlike the Constantinides volume, it does not annotate the books listed, but breaks them down into various categories to ease research.

SPECIAL READING SUGGESTIONS

U.S. Congress. Senate Select Committee to Study Governmental Operations with Respect to Intelligence Activities. Final Report and *Hearings, Book IV: Supplementary Detailed Staff Reports on Intelligence and Military Intelligence.* In other words, this is the Church Report, a thorough investigation of the CIA and other intelligence agencies, with testimony of witnesses who appeared before the Church Committee (Washington, D.C.: Government Printing Office, 1975-76).

The Clandestine Service of the Central Intelligence Agency, by Hans Moses. A study of the CIA's Directorate of Operations, published as a monograph in the series entitled *The Intelligence Profession*. Copies are available for $1.25 each by writing to the sponsor of the series, the Association of Former Intelligence Officers, 6723 Whittier Avenue, Suite 303-A, McLean, Virginia 22101.

Foreign Intelligence Literary Scene. This bimonthly newsletter/book review is edited by Thomas F. Troy and is invaluable to those who observe the literary intelligence scene. It reviews fiction and nonfiction, lists books, magazine articles, and newspaper accounts, and carries substantive reports on intelligence developments. Subscriptions are $25 per annum (University Publications of America, Inc., 44 North Market Street, Frederick, Maryland 21701).

ESPIONAGE FICTION

There are thousands of novels, in and out of print, about intelligence operations. Readable as they may be, thrillers of the Robert Ludlum variety are not authentic. For realistic accounts, read the novels of British writers Somerset Maugham, Graham Greene, and John Le Carré—all former intelligence officers. The two best American writers of espionage fiction are Charles McCarry and W.T. Tyler. McCarry is a former deep-cover agent for the CIA; Tyler (a pseudonym) rubbed shoulders with real spies in the Department of State's foreign service.